THE
LEAN
ADVANTAGE

Photo by Guy Appelman.

THE LEAN ADVANTAGE

by Clarence Bass

Clarence Bass' **RIPPED** ™Enterprises
Albuquerque, New Mexico

ISBN 0-9609714-2-4

Second Printing 1987

Published by Clarence Bass' Ripped Enterprises
528 Chama N.E.
Albuquerque, New Mexico 87108

Library of Congress Catalog Card No. 84-71083

Typesetting and Cover Design by Typography Unlimited
Albuquerque, New Mexico

Printed by Thomson-Shore, Inc.
Dexter, Michigan

Photograph on Back Cover by Wayne Gallasch

DEDICATION

I dedicate this book to Joe Weider, publisher of Muscle & Fitness *magazine, who makes the Ripped Department possible each month.*

ACKNOWLEDGEMENTS

My thanks to the staff at *Muscle & Fitness* magazine who edit the Ripped Department. I'm grateful for the extra polish they put on Ripped each month, and reviewing all of my columns for this book reminded me again of their outstanding contribution.

My wife, Carol, also contributes to the Ripped Department; she makes valuable suggestions and helps prepare my manuscript each month. She was my sounding board on this book as well. I couldn't get along without her faithful help and support.

TABLE OF CONTENTS

CONTENTS

DEDICATION
ACKNOWLEDGMENTS
INTRODUCTION: THE LEAN ADVANTAGE

INTRODUCTION: The Lean Advantage

Many people are concerned about being fat. They want the advantages—physical, emotional and social—of being lean, but they don't know how to go about it. Ninety percent of those who lose weight regain what they lost, and frequently more. They're convinced—wrongly—that getting lean and staying lean must involve suffering and deprivation. They spend a lifetime waging a losing battle against fat.

I'm not only convinced that the war on fat can be won, I believe it can be won without making yourself miserable in the process. The purpose of my Ripped column in *Muscle & Fitness* magazine is to explain the sensible way to lose fat and gain muscle. The Ripped Department is not only for those who want to be champion bodybuilders, it's also for those who simply want to know more about controlling their bodies.

My message doesn't have to be swallowed whole. In fact, I urge readers to take only what suits them and leave the rest. Questions and answers used in the column are selected for their broad application. They're intended to guide those who seek the ultimate in muscularity as well as those who only want to lose a few pounds of fat and keep it off.

Being lean has many advantages. People who are lean tend to be healthier. Dr. Kenneth Cooper says in his latest book, *The Aerobics Program for Total Well-Being,* that "carrying just five extra pounds... creates a deadlier drag than most people, including many physicians, now imagine." Being overweight contributes to many health problems, including heart disease, high blood pressure, stroke and diabetes. Furthermore, according to the American Cancer Society, obese people are definitely at greater risk of developing certain types of cancer than are people of normal weight. Of lesser concern, but still important, people who carry extra fat have lower energy levels; they can't get around as well as their leaner counterparts. I'm not a doctor so I don't stress medical problems in my column, but there's no denying the fact that obesity is a serious health problem.

The advantages of being lean are also psychological. You feel better about yourself when you're lean. You have more self-esteem and more self-confidence. You feel more in control of your body and your life, and you handle stress better. You feel better physically *and* emotionally.

What's more, you get along better in the social and business world when you're lean. Fat may be a non-issue in some societies, but in our society fat people are discriminated against. We're inclined to perceive lean people as more confident, energetic, competitive and self-reliant. If you're lean, you have an easier time getting a mate, a job and many other things.

Simply put, it pays to be lean—in many ways.

For four years now, through the Ripped Department, I've been explaining how proper diet, weight training and aerobic exercise combine to produce a stronger, healthier, leaner body. A review of the almost 50 columns I've written convinced me that they should be organized into one volume. The result is the book you now hold.

Readers tell me they enjoy and benefit from the Ripped Department each month. I believe you'll get even more out of reading all of the columns together. Read on and get the lean advantage.

CHAPTER ONE

BODY COMPOSITION TESTS

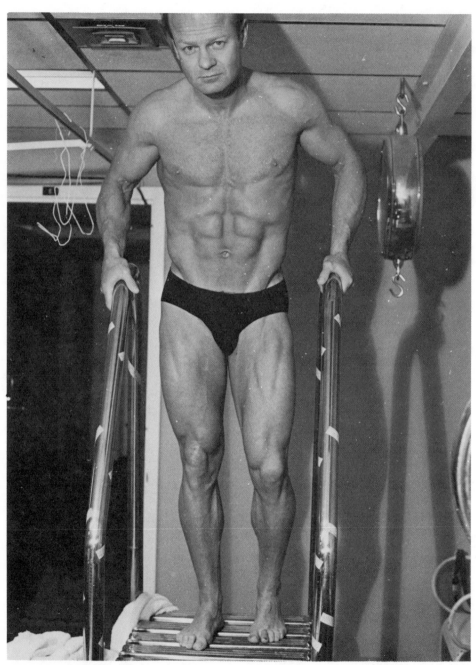

Here I'm getting ready to climb into the hydrostatic tank at Albuquerque's Lovelace Medical Center. I have my body composition measured regularly to help guide my training. *Photo by Denie.*

CHAPTER ONE: BODY COMPOSITION TESTS

Scales Don't Tell The Whole Story

Your bathroom scales don't tell you whether the weight you lost (or gained) is fat or muscle. And desirable changes can take place in your body while your weight remains unchanged. Your scales may indicate nothing is happening when, in fact, you're replacing fat with muscle. These are the circumstances where body composition tests can come to your aid.

Body composition tests help guide your training. At the outset, they tell you how much of your body weight is lean and how much is fat. Your mirror says whether you're too fat, and a body composition test gives you the details; it tells you how many pounds of fat you need to lose. After you embark on a diet and exercise program, further tests give you the feedback needed to zero in on your goal.

Since 1977, when I was first tested at Lovelace Medical Center, body composition tests have been a critical part of my training regimen. The tests tell me when I'm doing things right and, equally important, when I'm doing things wrong. I always keep an eye on the scales, but I never forget—and you shouldn't either—that body weight changes are made up of lean tissue and fat tissue. Rarely are gains all muscle or losses all fat. So, if you want the whole story on the results of your training, body composition tests are the answer.

Underwater Weighing

Q. I've read you have a very low percentge of body fat. How is this measured, and where can I get mine checked?

A. I've had my body composition measured 18 times in the last two-and-one-half years to guide me in my contest preparation. With the aid of the tests, I reduced my body fat to 2.4 percent for both the

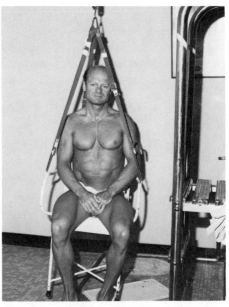

The underwater weighing procedure used by Albuquerque's Lovelace Medical Center is always the same. First they measure how much air I can blow out after taking a deep breath.

Next they weigh me out of water.

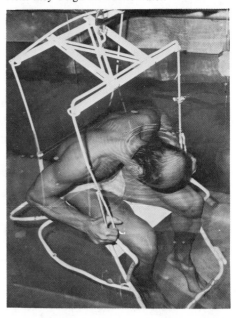

Once I'm in the tank and the water is still, I take a deep breath and slowly exhale into the mouth piece until they tell me to stop. That's Dr. Jack Loeppky and Treva Miller who have weighed me many times.

Finally, holding my breath, I slowly lower my head under the water and keep it there until they give me the signal to come up. *All photos by Bill Reynolds.*

1979 Past-40 Mr. USA and the Past-40 Mr. America contests.

To give you a frame of reference, the average man has 15 percent fat. Women average 25 percent. For men, 20 percent is considered obese; under 10 percent is lean. Top-class male marathon runners usually carry five or six percent fat.

The body needs some fat for the protection of internal organs and the proper functioning of nerve and brain tissue. Women need more fat than men. Even in a state of starvation, the body will retain some fat. For males a body fat level of three percent or lower is, in effect, "zero." The rock-bottom level for women is somewhat higher.

One of the most accurate methods for measuring body fat, and the one I use, is underwater weighing. (If you want the technical name, it's "hydrostatic weighing.") Your body weight out of water is compared to your weight completely submerged. The method is based on the fact that fat people are more buoyant than lean people. As you become leaner and more muscular, you become denser and heavier in relation to the water your body displaces. While a fat person floats like a beach ball, a lean person sinks like a cannon ball.

Most big universities have exercise physiology labs with hydrostatic tanks to perform body composition tests. I suggest that you contact the physical education department at the university nearest you and see if they have such facilities. Maybe you can arrange to be tested by students who are performing experiments that involve body composition testing. Under those circumstances, you probably won't be charged anything. If, on the other hand, they have to set up a special weighing, it could cost you $100, maybe more.

Fat Down/Muscle Up

Q. How many times has your body fat been measured?

A. My body composition has probably been measured more times than any other person's: I have now been tested a total of 46 times. The first time I was tested by underwater (hydrostatic) weighing was at Lovelace Medical Center in Albuquerque, New Mexico, on August 24th, 1977, and my body fat was measured at 2.4 percent. The last test was August 12th, 1983, and I again reached my personal record low of 2.4 percent body fat.

I am particularly pleased with this result, because my gross body weight is the highest it's ever been at that low body fat level. Since 1977, I have gained 9.06 pounds of body weight. In other words, I've gained slightly more than nine pounds of muscle while maintaining maximum leanness. Not bad, considering I'm 45 years old and have been training for more than 30 years.

According to body composition experts Drs. Frank I. Katch and William D. McArdle, the average man my age has a body fat level of about 25 percent. Five times over the last six years Lovelace Medical Center has measured my body fat level at 2.4 percent. That's lean!

NOTE:

See "Muscle After 45?" in Chapter Eleven and the graph in Chapter Five for the results of a later test performed on August 26th, 1983, which showed an additional muscle gain of 2.1 pounds and a further body fat reduction to one percent.

CHAPTER TWO

DIET:
THE BIG
PICTURE

CHAPTER TWO: DIET: THE BIG PICTURE
Get Ripped With A Balanced Diet

Q. You recommend that bodybuilders eat a well-balanced, low-calorie diet. A balanced diet might keep me healthy, but will it help me get ripped?

A. Obesity and poor nutrition go hand in hand. The empty-calorie, junk-food diet is unhealthy and fattening. A calorie-efficient, well-balanced diet is important for anyone striving to achieve a lean, strong, healthy body.

A balanced diet must have: (1) the proper carbohydrate/protein/fat ratio; (2) the proper calorie balance; and (3) foods from all the basic food groups.

A bodybuilder who wants to get ripped should pay special attention to the calorie intake and the preferred ratio of protein, carbohydrate and fat. Also, he or she should have a good general knowledge of the four basic food groups.

The idea of basic food groups took hold in the 1930s. Foods were placed in specific groups on the basis of similarities in nutrient content and the role of these foods in diet. At first, foods were grouped in the "Basic Eleven." However, this was too cumbersome, so the individual food groups were enlarged and the whole concept simplified until eventually the groups became our present "Basic Four."

The four basic food groups are the milk group, the meat group (which includes eggs, beans, peas and nuts), the fruit and vegetable group, and the bread and cereal group. You should eat four or more servings daily from the vegetable and fruit group and the bread and cereal group. Two or more servings a day are recommended from the milk and meat groups. In other words, to eat a balanced diet, two-thirds of your diet should come from grains, fruits and vegetables, and the remaining third from the milk and meat groups.

In his book *Diet and Nutrition,* Dr. Rudolph Ballentine observes that strikingly similar eating habits developed independently in

Two-thirds of a balanced diet should come from grains, fruits and vegetables, and the remaining third from the milk and meat groups. *Photo by Wayne Gallasch.*

Beans—all kinds—and rice are a regular part of the Bass family diet. *Photo by Wayne Gallasch.*

many parts of the world. The pattern that emerges is similar to the North American Basic Four, but with more emphasis on whole grains, beans and vegetables and less emphasis on dairy products and meat. Whole grains and—to a somewhat lesser degree—fresh vegetables, beans and other legumes make up the bulk of the traditional diets around the world. In these diets, dairy products, meat, fish and fowl are used mainly as seasoning. While the modern American diet relies on an animal-source main dish for protein, the traditional cultures studied by Dr. Ballentine derive their protein from a combination of grain and legumes. I favor the traditional emphasis on grains, legumes and vegetables because these foods are nourishing, filling and low calorie. The calorie breakdown in both the Basic Four food groups and the traditional diets studied by Ballentine is approximately 60 percent carbohydrate, 20 percent protein and 20 percent fat. This high carbohydrate/low protein diet ratio is much healthier for the bodybuilder than the low carbohydrate/high protein diet so many bodybuilders prefer.

Finally, we come to the critical issue of calorie intake. In the early 20th century the average adult male burned approximately 4,000 calories per day. Today the average man of the same size is far more sedentary and burns only 2,700 calories daily. Therefore, we must be careful to get a high nutrient return from the calories we consume.

Business administrators talk about the "cost effectiveness" of a product. Bodybuilders who are trying to get ripped should eat foods that are "calorie effective." In other words, he or she should steer towards foods high in nutrients but low in calories. The best way to be calorie effective is to stick with whole, natural foods that have all of the fiber and bulk left in them and no sugar or fat added. Whole grains, legumes, and fresh fruit and vegetables fill this calorie-effective category perfectly.

North Americans favor a "rich man's diet"—a diet high in animal protein and, therefore, high in fat. Fat has more than twice the calories of protein or carbohydrate. The calorie effective way to fill the 20 percent of the diet which should be protein is to reduce your intake of dairy products and meat, and eat more vegetable protein foods such as beans and peas. The protein/calorie ratio of rice and beans is 28 calories for each gram of protein—about the same as a T-bone steak. The difference is volume. A plateful of rice and beans (one cup rice and one-half cup beans) contains the same calories and protein as 2.5 ounces of T-bone steak. And a plateful of rice and beans is a lot more filling and satisfying than 2.5 ounces of T-bone steak.

When a bodybuilder is trying to get ripped, he or she should make every calorie count. The food you eat should be high in nutrition, low in calories and bulky enough to satisfy your hunger. You won't get a good return on your calorie expenditure with convenience and snack foods. They are invariably low in fiber and essential nutrients, and high in sugar and fat. In the supermarket, stick to the outside walls where the fruits, vegetables and dairy products are located. The only supermarket shelves you should be interested in are those which hold dried beans, peas, rice and whole grain items.

You can't beat the low-calorie balanced diet. It's the healthiest, most effective and pleasant way to get ripped.

Diet To Stay Lean

Q. In a recent issue of *Muscle & Fitness* you said that you keep your body fat around four percent throughout the year. What is your maintenance diet?

A. I stayed lean during all of 1980 and I'm continuing to do so in 1981. Meal by meal, this is what I usually eat:

For breakfast I have one egg, one-half piece of whole wheat toast, cereal and low-fat milk (two-thirds cup). The cereal consists of the following ingredients:

One cup cooked whole oats (oat groats)
Three tablespoons bran (see Update)
One tablespoon wheat germ
One tablespoon sunflower seeds
One tablespoon raisins

If I need to reduce calories I leave out the raisins and sunflower seeds. If I have to reduce more calories I also drop the egg and toast. To add calories I eat one more egg and more toast. I constantly adjust my diet depending on my body weight, how I look in the mirror and my regular body composition tests.

For lunch I have a peanut butter sandwich, a cup of plain, low-fat yogurt and a carrot, an apple or a pear. I rarely vary my lunch, but occasionally I will reduce the calories by cutting down on the amount of peanut butter in the sandwich. If I need to gain weight I may add an extra half of a peanut butter sandwich.

During the afternoon I usually snack on fruit, such as apples or pears. This keeps my blood sugar up and keeps me from getting too hungry.

My usual dinner is one cup cooked whole-grain brown rice, one-half cup cooked beans (pinto, black-eyed peas, lima, kidney or any other type of bean). I top the rice and beans with diced, cooked apple or pear and half to one cup of plain, low-fat yogurt. I also have a baked carrot on the side. This is a very filling meal and it tastes good, too. I really enjoy the natural sweetness of the cooked fruit and baked carrot. Later in the evening I usually have a snack consisting of one cup of low-fat milk, flavored with saccharine and vanilla extract, and thickened with an apple, pear or banana that's been put through a blender.

Depending on whether you want to gain, lose or maintain weight, you may find it necessary to eat more or less than I do. Your food intake will also vary depending on your metabolism and your activity level. You can determine the proper adjustments by keeping track of your body weight, watching how you look in the mirror and by having your body composition measured.

It's easy to stay lean if you understand the theory behind my diet. I emphasize natural foods that have all of the bulk and fiber left in them and no sugar or fat added. This allows me to feel full and satisfied without taking in excess calories.

If a contest, a photo session or a seminar isn't coming up, my wife Carol and I usually eat out about once a week. When we eat out I usually have a glass of wine, a big salad and a plain baked potato. If I'm really hungry I may also have fish or chicken and, if I feel the urge, dessert. Varying my diet for this one meal a week doesn't affect my body fat and it relieves any feeling of deprivation that I may have. This makes it easier to stick to my usual diet during the rest of the week.

Please, don't get the idea that you must eat the same foods that I do. Adjust the diet to suit yourself. If you emphasize natural foods, without any sugar, oil or butter added and without the fiber and bulk removed, you'll have no trouble staying lean.

UPDATE:

Since I wrote this column, I've stopped using bran. The phytic acid in bran binds minerals—calcium, zinc, iron and probably others—and carries them out of the body as waste. Too much bran can cause mineral deficiencies.

According to Jane Brody, personal health columnist for *The New York Times* and author of *Jane Brody's Nutrition Book,* this isn't likely to be a problem for most people, but it might be troublesome for adolescents, the elderly, and the poorly nourished, whose nutrient intake is borderline.

Sprinkling bran on everything is not the proper way to increase the fiber content of your diet. It's better to avoid fractionated foods like bran, and rely on whole cereal—whole wheat, whole rye, whole oats, et cetera—vegetables and fruit. Of course, you should also eat less of the nonfiber foods—sweets, meats and fats.

You Need Dietary Fat

Q. I have outlined a diet for myself that aims at a daily consumption of less than 35 grams of fat, about 15 percent of my daily caloric intake. If I want to enter a contest in the future and get "really ripped," I could cut my fat intake further. Do you think this would be advisable?

A. Many bodybuilders use a low-fat diet to increase muscularity, but it's important to realize that some dietary fat is necessary for good health. The essential fatty acid, linoleic acid, is indispensable to life and should be one or two percent of the calories we consume daily. Vegetable oils are a concentrated source of linoleic acid (but not coconut, palm or olive oil). The body can manufacture the other fats it needs. But like the essential amino acids, linoleic acid must be included in our food. The other two polyunsaturated fatty acids, arachidonic and linolenic, can be manufactured in the body from linoleic acid. Even strict low-fat diets such as the one recommended by Nathan Pritikin call for the equivalent of one tablespoon of polyunsaturated oil each day.

Pathologist Thomas J. Bassler has done more than 3,000 autopsies: He's concerned with what kills people. A runner himself, Bassler has made a special study of the unexpected deaths of about 30 very fit runners. He blames nutritional arrhythmia, an irregular heartbeat caused by the lack of something in the diet. His theory is that these high-mileage runners restricted their dietary fat intake so severely that they did not get the linoleic acid they needed. Bassler recommends wheat germ, nuts, seeds and whole grains along with some milk and eggs as good sources for linoleic acid. The deaths that Dr. Bassler studied are rare, about six a year, but they dramatically illustrate the need for fat in the diet. Dr. Bassler also says that lack of dietary fat was responsible for the well-publicized deaths of several obese individuals on liquid protein diets.

Dietary fat is also needed for the assimilation of fat-soluble vitamins A, D, E and K, which don't mix with water. Dietary fat transports them into the body and through the walls of the digestive tract. On the lighter side, a little fat makes food taste better. It also helps satisfy your appetite, because fats leave the stomach slowly, delaying the return of hunger.

Restricting your fat intake is very effective for weight reduction, because fat contains about nine calories per gram compared to four in carbohydrates or protein. Most Americans, including the majority of bodybuilders, eat far more fat than necessary. Excessive dietary fat not only contributes to obesity but is also implicated in health problems, including heart disease and cancer.

The Senate's Select Committee on Nutrition and Human Needs recommended in 1977 that Americans reduce their total fat intake, saturated and unsaturated, from 42 percent of daily calories to 30 percent. Jane Brody, personal health columnist of *The New York Times,* in *Jane Brody's Nutrition Book* says that one can safely reduce fat intake to 10 percent of daily calories—28 grams in a 2,500-calorie diet. She also recommends the use of vegetable oils in place of hard shortenings and animal fat.

So you're on the right track by limiting your dietary fat intake, but you should not cut your intake below 10 percent of your daily calories. So long as you include some foods with linoleic acid in your diet you'll be okay.

Personally, I get my essential fat from whole grains, bread, seeds and nuts. And I almost always include milk and eggs in my diet; but I usually pour the cream off my milk, and I rarely eat more than one egg a day. I eat very little meat because of its high fat content, and I don't use butter, oil or mayonnaise for the same reason.

It's not necessary to go to dietary extremes to get "really ripped." Watch your fat intake carefully, but don't try to completely eliminate fat from your diet. A low-calorie, balanced diet is the way to get ripped. Moderation is the best policy for becoming lean and staying that way.

New Evidence on Protein Needs

The National Research Council and nutrition experts such as Dr. Nathan J. Smith, author of *Food for Sport,* have long told us that exercise doesn't significantly increase the need for dietary protein. Now, however, new evidence suggests that the bodybuilder's gut feeling that he or she needs more protein may be correct. *The Physician and Sportsmedicine* (Vol. 11, No. 7, July, 1983) has published findings that "Currently recommended maximum protein requirements may not be adequate for physically active individuals." That's big news for doctors and athletes alike.

Scientists still say that high-intensity exercise doesn't tear down muscle tissue so no extra protein is needed to rebuild muscle following exercise. (Exercise depletes the glycogen stored in the muscles.) Muscle building is a slow process, and only a little more than the usual amount of protein is required for muscle-building purposes. There's no change on that point. What has changed is that the new research suggests protein provides a significant portion of the total calories used during exercise. That's important, because heretofore protein requirements have been based on the needs of resting persons, not people who are physically active.

Specifically, the researchers found that almost 90 percent of the current estimated requirement for the essential amino acid leucine was used during a two-hour ride on a stationary bicycle at 55 percent of maximum work capacity. Furthermore, the data suggests that increased energy expenditure can cause an even greater rise in leucine oxidation.

The bottom line is that no one knows exactly how much protein physically active individuals like bodybuilders need. Nevertheless, the conventional view that exercise doesn't increase the need for dietary protein has been severely shaken.

My guess is that bodybuilders need a little more than the one gram of protein per 2.2 pounds of bodyweight recommended by the National Research Council. Still, don't go overboard on protein. Extra protein, like extra calories from any source, builds fat, not muscle.

Vitamin & Mineral Supplements

Q. Is it necessary to take vitamin and mineral supplements when following the balanced diet that you recommend for getting ripped?

A. My father, a medical doctor, gave me vitamin and mineral supplements when I was a child. I have taken them all of my life.

Over the years I've learned that vitamin and mineral supplementation is advisable, especially when getting ripped. If we lived in a world free of pollution and stress, if we had an active lifestyle, and ate an abundant variety of fresh, natural foods, supplements probably wouldn't be necessary. Unfortunately, most of us live stress-filled lives in a polluted environment. We're sedentary most of the day and often eat foods which have been robbed of nutrients by processing, storage and shipping. Taking vitamin and mineral supplements can help us overcome stress, inadequate nutrition and pollution.

When reducing calories to get ripped it's easy to shortchange yourself on vitamins and minerals. Within the calorie limits you set for yourself, fill your basic nutrient needs with a balanced diet of fresh, unprocessed foods. Don't make the mistake of trying to live on supplements. It would be a foolish gamble to believe that scientists have enough knowledge to make supplements that include all nutrients essential to robust health. Good, wholesome food should be the cornerstone of your diet. Supplements are simply additional insurance.

I take a high-potency complete vitamin and mineral supplement. I prefer a formula which divides the recommended daily dose into several capsules or tablets to be taken with meals throughout the day. Vitamin and mineral supplements prepackaged in one daily dose, however, are convenient and especially handy while traveling. In addition, I take a vitamin C formula to aid tissue repair and protect against infection, a vitamin E formula to promote better blood circulation and as an antioxidant, a B-complex formula to protect against stress and aid in protein, fat and carbohydrate metabolism. I also take a chelated mineral formula, and I recommend that bodybuilders take a liver concentrate because unknown agents, vital to health, are thought to be stored in the liver.

Don't try to get the extra vitamin C, B, E and minerals by taking several times the recommended dose of the vitamin and mineral formula. If you do, you may take toxic amounts of vitamins A or D.

If you wish to dig deeper into the subject of vitamin and mineral supplementation, I recommend you read Richard Passwater's two books, *Super Nutrition* and *Super Nutrition for Healthy Hearts.*

Heavy Into Starvation

Q. I have to tell you a comment I heard about you recently. A 17-year-old girl in my dance class has recently taken up bodybuilding in a local gym. I asked her if she'd heard of you. "Oh, yes," she said, "he's heavy into starvation." Obviously she knows you have a very low percentage of body fat, but I believe she's misinformed about your methods. Do you care to comment?

A. Yes, it seems to be a common misconception that bodybuilders must starve themselves to reach peak condition. It's true that some bodybuilders consume as few as 800 calories a day before a contest, but that's a mistake. The purpose of a precontest diet is to burn the body's fat as food. The fat cells provide energy for activity, but they don't provide all the nutrients the body needs to function properly. When you starve yourself you begin to use your body tissue for fuel—not simply fat, but muscle and blood stores as well. In addition, starvation diets reduce your energy level so much that you can't train properly. This causes an additional loss of muscle.

I never starve myself, even to get down to a 2.4 percent body fat level. The way to achieve a minimum of fat with a maximum of muscle is to slowly reduce your body fat. Never try to lose more than one pound of fat a week. Reduce your caloric intake slightly and increase your activity level slightly. That's the healthy way to get ripped. It's also the best way to win contests.

To Bulk Or Not To Bulk?

Q. I've reduced my bodyweight to 190 pounds, but I'm still a little flabby. The people who run the gym where I train tell me to eat more, gain weight and fill out. They also tell me to eat more red meat. If I gain weight slowly and fill out, will I lose my flab? Or should I diet and lose more weight and then fill out? My training is coming along great. I'm really starting to pick up on the amount of weight I'm using, but I'm hearing so many opinions I'm getting confused.

A. If my body composition tests have taught me anything—and I've been tested 37 times in the last five years—it's that gaining muscle and fat, bulking up, is a mistake. It takes very few additional calories to gain muscle because muscle is 70 percent water and is gained very slowly.

On the rare occasions when I do try to gain weight, I consume no more than 100-200 extra calories per day, approximately the number found in one or two eggs. Eating more than that almost always results in a fat gain. When you gain fat along with muscle, the muscle you gain will probably be lost when you reduce your weight to your desired level.

The best strategy for a bodybuilder is to first reduce his or her body fat to a minimum level, and then gain muscle slowly, without gaining fat. The fact that your poundages increased while you lost weight means you're gaining muscle while you lose fat. That's difficult for most people to do, so you're doing fine.

Eating more red meat won't help, either. The idea of eating red meat to build muscle comes, I suppose, from the ancient idea of eating the flesh of animals that possess desirable attributes, for instance, eating the heart of a lion to gain courage. In more modern terms, the idea is that eating muscle, red meat, will help you build muscle. The problem is that red meat is mainly fat. For example, only 20 percent of the calories in a T-bone steak are protein; the remaining 80 percent are fat. If you're going to eat meat it would be much better to eat chicken or fish. The protein in chicken is as good as that in steak, but chicken (without skin) is 64 percent protein and only 31 percent fat. For tuna (with the oil drained) 58 percent of the calories are protein and 37 percent fat. Filet of sole is even leaner—90 percent protein and only 10 percent fat.

Personally, I eat every little meat, including fish and chicken. The protein in eggs and milk is better balanced and more usable than the protein in red meat, fish or chicken. In addition to milk and eggs, I get the protein I need from vegetable sources like peas, beans, nuts and seeds. However, the main reason I eat little meat is that it slows the movement of food through the intestines because it doesn't contain fiber. Digestion and elimination function better without meat.

Athletes, including bodybuilders, don't need meat. Muscles use carbohydrates and fats, not protein, for fuel. Steve Reeves, former Mr. America Roy Hilligen, former Mr. International Andreas Cahling, and four-time Mr. Universe Bill Pearl are ovolactovegetarians. They eat eggs and dairy products, but little or no red meat, fish or chicken. Bill Pearl says, "There is absolutely no question that it is possible to build a high class physique and be a vegetarian at the same time." Pearl knows what he's talking about. He's built himself up to over 240 pounds with good muscularity—without eating meat.

The Results of Diet Without Exercise

Q. The thing that impresses me most about you is your chin; you don't have a trace of a double chin. I went on a diet and lost 50 pounds. Then I took up weight training to firm up my body. I've stayed at the reduced weight and trained hard and consistently for over a year, but I still have a double chin. How can I get rid of it?

A. I've been complimented on a lot of things, but never my chin. At first I thought you were joking, but after thinking about it I realized that many people, men and women, young and old, do have an extra chin they'd like to lose. After all, you can't hide your chin and neck. They're always on public display.

In your case, your first mistake was waiting until after your weight loss to take up weight training. Gross weight loss (the loss measured by your bathroom scales) is important, but far more important is fat loss. Most people assume that the weight they lose on a diet is fat. That's an erroneous assumption. Diet alone usually results in a loss of muscle tissue as well—50 percent or more of the weight reduction may be lean tissue. Your 50-pound weight loss may have included 25 or more pounds of muscle. This resulted in loose skin on many parts of your body, including your neck right below your chin.

Exercise physiologists have proven conclusively through body composition tests that exercise along with diet increases fat loss and reduces muscle loss. My own experiments have shown this to be particularly true when the exercise is weight training. A properly designed weight training program, more than any other type of exercise, stimulates all the muscles of the body. It protects and maintains muscle tissue while you lose fat. Diet plus exercise, particularly weight training, is far superior to diet alone.

So, like thousands of others, you made the mistake of dieting without exercise and you're left with a double chin. What should you do now? I recommend that you add some neck exercises to your weight training program to fill out and tone the area under your chin.

You can buy a neck strap at most sporting goods stores. They usually come with an illustrated course explaining how to exercise all parts of your neck. Keep up your weight training, continue your diet, and use the head strap to zero in on your neck muscles. Before you know it, you'll have only one chin.

CHAPTER THREE

FOCUS ON SPECIFIC FOODS

CHAPTER THREE: FOCUS ON SPECIFIC FOODS

Milk

Q. I hear a lot of bodybuilders say they don't drink milk because it makes you smooth. What do you think?

A. That's nonsense! It's excess calories that make you smooth— not any specific food. It's true, however, that some people can't digest milk. Those with this problem may find they can tolerate yogurt or hard cheeses. But if you can digest milk, there's no reason to exclude it from a definition diet. Milk is one of the most nourishing and balanced foods. Taken in moderation, it won't make you smooth. I always include milk in my diet, even right before a contest.

Milk Okay, But...

Q. Do you still drink milk? I continue to hear bodybuilders say that milk makes them smooth.

A. In my book *Ripped,* I said, "If you can digest milk, there's no reason to exclude it from a reducing diet." That's still true, but I've added an exception which I'll come back to shortly.

According to *Jane Brody's Nutrition Book* (W.W. Norton & Company, 1981), "On an item-by-item basis cow's milk contains nearly all the nutrients needed to maintain life and support growth." Unlike meat and eggs, which have only fat and protein, milk is a good source of protein, fats and carbohydrates. Milk is an excellent source of calcium. Two cups supply three-quarters of the daily calcium requirement for adults. Fortified milk is our main dietary source of vitamin D (milk contains no vitamin D naturally). Milk really is close to being a perfect food. Its main nutritional shortcoming is that it doesn't contain enough iron.

True, milk is high in fat. I purchase my milk from a dairy; it's not

Except for the last several days before a contest or photo session, I drink two to four cups of milk almost every day. *Photo by Bill Reynolds.*

homogenized and has the cream on the top. When I'm trying to reduce my body fat, I pour the cream down the drain. This reduces the calories from 150 to under 100 per cup and has little effect on nutritional value otherwise. Milk, in moderation, won't make you fat. I consume a quart of milk or yogurt almost every day.

From the bodybuilding standpoint, milk's main shortcoming is its sodium content. Sodium controls the volume of fluids inside and outside of the body's cells. Sodium concentrates in the fluid outside of the cells and when it's present in excess pulls water from the cells into the spaces outside the cells. This can make an otherwise lean and muscular physique look bloated and puffy. Indeed, sodium can make a bodybuilder smooth; and this is the basis for my exception to the "milk is okay" rule.

According to Ellington Darden, Ph.D., who did post-doctoral research in food and nutrition at Florida State University and is currently Director of Research for Nautilus Sports/Medical Industries, the minimum daily requirement for sodium is 200 mg— the amount in one-tenth teaspoon of salt.

One cup of whole milk contains 120 milligrams of sodium. The quart of milk I usually drink each day contains more than twice the minimum daily requirement for sodium and when taken with the other foods I eat—sodium is present in almost all foods—may be enough to slightly blur my definition. For this reason, I no longer drink milk during the last several days before a photo session or contest. That's the only time I abstain from milk. Compared to a McDonald's Big Mac with 1,150 milligrams of sodium, or a Kentucky Fried Chicken dinner with 2,128 milligrams, milk is quite low in sodium.

So there is some truth to the bodybuilding belief that milk will make you smooth. Nevertheless, if you like milk and can digest it— many people can't—I recommend it even when you're reducing. Competitive bodybuilders should eliminate milk immediately before a contest, however.

Peanut Butter Sandwiches

Q. Is it really true that you get cut eating peanut butter sandwiches?

A. I've been asked this question repeatedly since it was reported in the June issue of *Muscle & Fitness* that before a contest my lunch includes a peanut butter sandwich with lots of peanut butter and two slices of bread. Actually, I've been eating peanut butter sandwiches for lunch year-round since 1977. And my body fat has been measured at 2.4 percent three times—June 9, 1977; August 9, 1979, and September 12, 1979. During this past year my body fat hovered around 3.1 percent. The highest it climbed all year was 4.8 percent on February 14, 1980.

I was more ripped than ever for recent photo sessions supervised by Joe Weider. Many at Gold's Gym said they had never seen anyone more ripped than I was at the time Joe had me photographed. Obviously, peanut butter sandwiches have not made me fat, and I'll tell you why.

First, I like peanut butter sandwiches, and it's convenient to take one with me to my law office for lunch. I control my calories all year long, and it's easier to keep track if I pack my lunch rather than eat it in a restaurant. Like most processed foods, regular supermarket peanut butter has sugar and salt added. Sugar adds calories and salt causes water retention, so my wife gets our peanut butter at a health food store. It contains nothing but roasted peanuts. She also buys our bread there, selecting the lowest calorie whole grain variety available.

Like any other high-calorie food, too much peanut butter would make me fat, but a measured amount of the kind I eat is okay. If you use your head and practice moderation, you can eat almost anything you want and still stay ripped.

Peanut Butter Sandwich Revisited

Q. I've just read in your book *Ripped 2* that you usually have a peanut butter sandwich for lunch. Peanut butter is loaded with fat and calories (approximately 160 per ounce). Why do you eat it when you're trying to stay lean?

A. Regular readers of this column know that I've been eating peanut butter for lunch since 1977. I almost always lunch on peanut butter on whole wheat bread, plain low-fat yogurt and fruit or a raw carrot. I like peanut butter, and at lunchtime it's a convenient

I make my own peanut butter in a food processor; but sometimes I eat the peanuts for lunch plain—two tablespoons, roasted and unsalted. *Photo by Wayne Gallasch.*

sandwich to make at my office. It's easier to keep track of my calories if I have lunch at my desk rather than in a restaurant.

You're right—peanut butter is high in fat and calories, and you will get fat if you eat too much. But one reason I'm able to control my calories and stay lean is I make it a point to eat foods I like. One sure way to blow your diet is to try to eat low-calorie foods that you find boring and tasteless.

I'm careful not to go overboard on peanut butter or any other high-calorie food. Regular supermarket peanut butter, like most processed foods, has sugar and salt added. Sugar adds calories and excess salt causes water retention, so I make my own peanut butter in the food processor. I use nothing but raw peanuts—no sugar and no salt. And most importantly, I eat only one sandwich with a measured amount of peanut butter. I avoid the temptation of eating more by putting the jar back in the refrigerator before I sit down to eat. The only food in front of me is the food I plan to eat.

While I have eaten basically the same thing for lunch for the past six years—uniform eating is another of my secrets for controlling calories and staying lean—I'm always on the lookout for ways to improve my diet. I've recently found a way to cut the calories in my peanut butter sandwich without reducing eating enjoyment.

I had heard about tofu (soybean curd), but until recently I had shied away from it because I didn't know much about it. But the August, 1983 issue of *Today's Living* featured a recipe that combined tofu and peanut butter. About the same time I also read the U.S. Department of Agriculture recommends peanut-butter-vegetable sandwiches. Needless to say, this gave me ideas for improving my lunchtime menu.

Tofu is low in fat, high in protein, and four ounces contain only 82 calories. As you point out, one ounce of peanut butter has 160 calories. Tofu has a nice bland taste. It reduces calories and adds nutritional value to almost any recipe and, significantly, it doesn't impair the flavor of the final product.

The recipe in *Today's Living* calls for 12 ounces tofu, one-half cup peanut butter, one-and-one-half bananas, two tablespoons lemon juice and one-two tablespoons honey. I simplified the recipe by leaving out the banana, lemon juice and honey. I just reduced the amount of peanut butter in my sandwich and added a slice of tofu. It's a delicious way to cut calories.

The USDA suggests adding shredded cabbage, chopped celery

and chopped raisins to peanut butter. I haven't tried that yet, but it sounds like a good idea. Shredded carrots would also be a tasty way to reduce the calories in a peanut butter sandwich.

Readers like you who are concerned about the amount of fat and calories in my lunchtime favorite should try a peanut butter-tofu or peanut butter-vegetable sandwich instead. You'll be able to satisfy your taste for peanut butter and, at the same time, curb your caloric intake.

Bread is Good Diet Food

Q. I read recently that when you decide to reduce one of the first things you should eliminate from your diet is bread. Is that correct?

A. That's a common misconception. Actually bread, especially high-fiber bread, is one of the best diet foods. Dr. Olaf Mickelson and his colleagues at Michigan State University have shown that college students lost weight eating whatever they wanted if they ate 12 slices of low-calorie, high-fiber bread each day. The bread made them feel full and reduced their hunger for other foods.

I never eliminate bread from my diet. I usually eat four or more slices of bran bread every day, even when I'm making a maximum effort to reduce. Butter and jelly are no-no's, but bread itself is A-OKAY.

Meatless Diets: Humans Are Natural Vegetarians

Q. I notice that you don't eat meat. Why not?

A. I stopped eating meat seven or eight years ago after reading Dr. David Reuben's book *The Save Your Life Diet,* which details the advantages of the high-fiber diet. Since then I have eaten meat, fish or chicken, but only on occasion. I've found that I feel better when I don't eat meat.

When I occasionally eat meat, fish or chicken, my weight goes up and I feel a fullness for several days afterward. This is because flesh foods contain little fiber and slow down digestion and elimination. They cause constipation.

There's a good reason why I feed my German shepherd, Sam, meat though I rarely eat it myself. Carnivorous animals—including

50

the dog, lion, wolf, cat, et cetera—are made to eat meat. Their teeth are long and sharp for cutting the meat, and they have a smooth, short digestive tract—only three times the length of their bodies—which allows them to digest meat and get rid of the waste products rapidly. Flesh decays quickly and the products of this decay can be harmful to the body. On the other hand, the human digestive system is more like that of plant-eating animals, including the cow, elephant, sheep, llama and anthropoid ape. The teeth are better designed for grinding than cutting, and the intestines are long and convoluted, allowing us to digest high-fiber plant foods, which take a long time to be broken down and absorbed. Our molars are for grinding our food and, like the ape, our digestive system is 12 times the length of our body. The human digestive tract retains the toxic waste products of flesh foods in the body far longer than is the case with carnivores.

Julian M. Whitaker, M.D., founder and director of The National Heart and Diabetes Treatment Institute, Inc., in Huntington Beach, California, says, "Human beings clearly are not carnivorous by physiology—our anatomy and digestive system show that we must have evolved for millions of years living on fruits, nuts, grain and vegetables." Harvard Medical nutritionist Mark Hegsted agrees: "I think man developed on a largely vegetarian, plant-food diet. Our bodies are not designed to eat a diet high in fat and animal products."

Phil Donahue recently devoted an entire segment of his TV program to vegetarian eating. I was quite interested to hear him say that only a few years ago he thought vegetarians were a little strange, but that he has since learned better. He observed cardiologists almost unanimously agree that we would be better off if we ate less meat. The meatless diet probably also protects against cancer.

In her book *The New York Times Guide to Personal Health,* Jane Brody points out that international studies show that people who develop colon-rectal cancer consume more meat than those who are free of this disease. For example, the Japanese—who don't consume much meat—suffer far less from this form of cancer than we do in the United States.

It's important for bodybuilders to understand that they don't need to eat meat to fulfill their protein requirement. As I state in my book *Ripped 2,* our protein needs can be supplied by vegetable sources. True, vegetable sources of protein are less complete and less efficiently used by the body than animal proteins, but that isn't a concern if you drink milk or eat eggs. Eggs and dairy products combine with vegetable proteins in a way that makes them complete. That's why I include one cup of milk or yogurt, or an egg, with each of my main meals.

Finally, it's easier for me to control my calorie consumption if I avoid meat, because bulky, vegetable protein foods are more filling. For example, a plateful of rice and beans (one cup rice, one-half cup beans) contains approximately the same calories and protein as 2.5 ounces of steak. Also a plateful of rice and beans is a lot more satisfying and filling than 2.5 ounces of steak. Simply put, I get more eating pleasure per calorie when I eat less meat and more fruits, vegetables and grains.

Watch Your Salt Intake

Q. Getting ripped is just a matter of losing body fat, right?

A. Wrong. A salty appetizer in an Acapulco restaurant almost cost Mike Mentzer the 1978 Mr. Universe contest. Cottage cheese had the same type of effect on my physique at the 1980 Past-40 Mr. America contest in Atlanta.

In his *Heavy Duty Journal,* Mike Mentzer relates how his condition went from razor sharp to waterlogged and puffy as a result of carelessness while he was enjoying a dinner with Joe and Betty Weider the night before the contest. Later he found out he'd made a mistake when Frank Zane, who was doing the TV commentary for CBS, ran backstage and asked him what he'd done to lose his cuts.

In my case, the cottage cheese was so ruinous to my definition that the first thing my wife said to me after the pre-judging was: "What happened to your cuts?"

Even though one's body fat is very low, as mine was in Atlanta, and as Mike Mentzer's was in Acapulco, salt and water can destroy your physique. You can go from supercut to smooth overnight.

In Atlanta, I ate most of my meals from the salad bar buffet in the hotel. But I substituted cottage cheese for my usual yogurt. I learned the hard way that cottage cheese has eight times as much salt as plain yogurt. One cup of creamed cottage cheese contains 850 milligrams of sodium, while one cup of plain yogurt contains only 105 milligrams of sodium. Salt (sodium chloride) holds water in the body and causes that water to collect in the spaces between the cells. This creates a puffy and bloated appearance.

Physique contestants should familiarize themselves with the sodium content of foods. Most foods served in restaurants are heavily salted, and most processed and prepared foods contain added salt. For example, 3½ ounces of fresh, raw peas contain only two milligrams of sodium, but the same amount of processed, canned peas has 236 milligrams of sodium. Before a contest or a photo session I now make it a point to stick with unprocessed natural foods and avoid unfamiliar foods. I don't put anything in my mouth unless I know its sodium content.

Most people eat more salt than they need. There is no established dietary requirement for sodium because the mineral is present in almost all foods. I never add salt to anything, and I think that's a good rule for most people to follow. Dieters in particular should be careful of their salt intake. I've often noticed a gain of two or three pounds after eating in a restaurant—even though my calorie consumption was not excessive. That weight gain is caused by salt. Dieters who want the scales to reward them for sticking to their diet should avoid salt.

Yes, low body fat is important, but to be ripped, you must also rid your body of excess water. Seemingly innocent dietary changes the last day or two before a contest can ruin months of preparation. To achieve super sharp, ripped condition, you must lose all excess body fat and body water.

Alcohol and Weight Control

Q. I'm a workaholic in a high pressure job and enjoy having a Scotch before dinner and a glass or two of wine with my meal. I'm physically active and train regularly with weights. My problem is I'm too bulky. I've decided to trim down. If necessary, I can stop drinking. What are your thoughts on alcohol and weight control?

A. After a day at my law office, I too would like a glass or two of wine with my dinner, but I find it's best if I don't have any. Alcohol adds calories, but that's not the main reason I skip the wine. Alcohol weakens the control I usually have over my appetite. It seems to anesthetize my stomach and encourage me to go on eating beyond the point where I would normally be full and satisfied.

I work out in the evening after I eat. If I have wine with my meals and particularly if I overeat too, I want to go to sleep instead of train. I handle alcohol just like I do dessert. I only have it on special occasions—usually when my wife and I go to a restaurant for dinner. Then, I usually have only one glass of wine even though I might like more.

You'll stay on your diet better if you don't have alcohol with your meals. To relax and wind down after a pressure-packed day at work, hit the weights, not the bottle.

Beer For Bodybuilders?

Q. Most of the men at the gym where I train are heavy beer drinkers, and they don't seem to be suffering any negative effects. Is beer a good beverage for bodybuilders? I recently cut back on my beer consumption and now I'm wondering if this was necessary.

A. Beer is both an intoxicant and a food. Alcohol is absorbed directly through the walls of the stomach and is, therefore, a quick source of energy. Some long-distance runners claim drinking beer before and even during a race actually improves performance. In addition to providing fluids and ready calories, limited amounts of beer can be a stimulant.

For a bodybuilder, a cold beer may be refreshing after a hard workout. You say, however, that your gym friends are "heavy beer drinkers." I think that spells trouble. In moderation, beer may be fine for bodybuilders. However, a 12-ounce can of beer contains about 150 calories, and excess calories will lead to an increase in body fat. The last thing a bodybuilder needs is a beer belly.

NOTE:

It's not true that alcohol calories don't count, because all alcohol consumed is burned by the liver and, therefore, none is left for energy storage as fat. The fact that alcohol calories are not stored as fat doesn't mean that you can't get fat from drinking extra calories in the form of alcohol. Your body simply stores more of the other foods you eat as fat. If you consume more calories than you burn— as food *or* drink—the excess will turn up on your body as fat.

Coffee

Q. Some diet books encourage coffee drinking. Do you recommend coffee as a means of controlling appetite?

A. I didn't drink coffee at all until a few years ago, when I started drinking it at the office as a mental stimulant. Then I developed the "coffee habit" and was drinking many cups each day. By chance, I happened to have a blood test taken on a day when I had been drinking coffee heavily. When I got back to the office, the lab technician called and asked me how I was feeling. He said my blood sugar was abnormally low, so low that I could have hypoglycemia. It then occurred to me that I usually got more tired and shaky as the day wore on; I suspected coffee was the cause. So I cut back on coffee, and my blood sugar has been normal ever since.

Everybody knows the caffeine in coffee is a stimulant. It stimulates your brain and raises your basal metabolic rate. It may suppress your appetite, but only temporarily, because the caffeine also triggers the release of insulin, which causes your blood sugar to drop, and that makes you feel hungry again.

In addition to being a mental stimulant, caffeine lessens fatigue and increases the capacity of your muscles to work. For this reason, coffee taken about 30 minutes before a workout can be helpful.

I drink coffee in the morning to wake up and before workouts, but otherwise I rarely drink it. I don't recommend coffee as an appetite suppressant. Coffee may take your mind off food for a while, but you're soon hungrier than you were before.

CHAPTER FOUR

TIPS FOR SUCCESSFUL DIETING

CHAPTER FOUR: TIPS FOR SUCCESSFUL DIETING

Lose Slowly

Q. I weigh a flabby 210. My doctor says I must lose at least 40 pounds. My goal is to lose weight fast. I get discouraged when I diet a week and lose only one or two pounds. I want to lose at least five pounds a week. How can I break out of this prison of fat?

A. I understand the urgency you feel, but rushing the reducing process is the worst thing you can do. Setting your goals too high will guarantee failure. It took you a while to put on those 40 pounds and it will take a while to lose them. Realistic goals plus patience and persistence will insure success.

To lose one pound of fat, you must burn 3,500 calories. To lose five pounds a week, you would have to burn 17,500 calories, or 2,500 each day. That's too much. You'd have to starve yourself—literally. You couldn't stay on such a diet very long and certainly not long enough to lose 40 pounds. You'll find it relatively easy, however, to create a deficit of 750 calories a day and lose 1.5 pounds a week.

Don't be discouraged at what I suggest. Losing 1.5 pounds a week will take you to your goal of weighing 170 pounds in only six months. While 1.5 pounds of fat may not seem like much, it's really a lot. To get an idea, go to the grocery store and look at a 1.5-pound package of hamburger. Since meat is denser than fat, a 1.5-pound package of fat would be much bigger.

You can create a daily 750-calorie deficit through a combination of increased activity and reduced food intake. By walking a mile, you burn 100 calories. By walking 1.5 miles at a comfortable pace each morning and each evening, you'll burn 300 extra calories a day. Cut the additional 450 calories through diet. A calorie counter book will show you that eating 450 fewer calories each day is easy. Cutting two slices of bread and two cups of milk will do it. If you're into junk food, it will be even easier. One sugared doughnut contains about 230 calories. Drop junk food and substitute unprocessed, natural foods. Stress fresh fruits, vegetables and whole grain products. They're more filling than processed foods and contain far fewer calories.

Be patient, persistent, and systematic. Before you know it, you'll be free from your prison of fat.

Weigh Yourself Daily

Q. How often do you think someone trying to get ripped should weigh himself or herself?

A. I weigh myself every day. Most of the diet books say this is a mistake because you may become discouraged if your weight doesn't come down each day. These books usually recommend weekly weighing. They're correct that your weight probably won't drop every day, even if you stay on your diet, while it will drop on a week-to-week basis. But a bodybuilder should become familiar with what's happening to his or her body on a daily basis. He or she needs constant feedback on the body's reaction to different foods. For example, a bodybuilder should know that salty foods cause water-weight gain and a puffy, bloated look; that meat slows down the digestive process and causes constipation and weight gain; and that a low-carbohydrate, high-protein diet causes dehydration. Daily weighing makes you aware of all these changes.

If you understand the story the scales tell, you'll be better able to control your body. You won't become discouraged because you'll know why your weight is changing or not changing. If you overeat and gain several pounds, you'll realize the gain is mainly water weight and, therefore, temporary.

One reminder: For a true comparison, bodyweight must be recorded at the same time each day. Your weight fluctuates during the day, usually recording lowest in the morning. I weigh myself as soon as I get up each day.

Daily weighing has never failed to produce the weight gain or loss I project for myself. By adjusting my food intake and my activity in response to the daily record of my weight, I invariably gain or lose precisely at the rate I plan. I recommend daily weighing year-round.

I weigh myself when I get up every day, year-round. *Photo by Bill Reynolds.*

Moderate Evening Eating Is Okay

Q. Is it true that eating in the evening when your activity level is low will result in fat buildup?

A. Heart specialist Dr. George Sheehan, the runner-philosopher who wrote the best-seller *Running and Being,* says that for him, "Obesity starts at 6:00 P.M."

By early evening, the most active part of the day is over for most people. They've had dinner and they're home with the TV and the refrigerator. One snack leads to another. So from the standpoint of time on your hands and the availability of food, the evening hours are dangerous.

It's not true, however, that food eaten after 7:00 or 8:00 p.m. will be deposited as fat necessarily. It doesn't make much difference when you eat so long as you don't eat more calories than you burn.

I routinely have a snack at 9:00 or 9:30 p.m. My snack is planned. I know exactly what I'm going to have. I look forward to it. The snack satisfies me and I'm not tempted to garbage up on anything else.

Plan your meals and spread them out throughout the day. There's no need to wire your jaw shut at 7:00 p.m.

UPDATE:

A recent study conducted at Cornell University found that exercising 45 minutes after a meal burned off 10 to 15 percent more calories than did the same activity on an empty stomach. The same study found that students who exercised the day after they had overeaten burned off more calories than they did doing the same exercise when they had not overeaten. It seems that exercise helps the body to "waste" excess calories.

The Cornell study suggests it's not a good idea to overeat in the evening; and if you do, exercising the following morning will help. Still, the best policy is to eat moderately throughout the day.

Spread Meals Throughout The Day

Q. I've read that eating one big meal and fasting the rest of the day is a good way to lose weight. Is this true?

A. No, it's better to spread your calories out over the day in several small meals. A study on rats shows why. Two groups of rats were fed the same low-calorie diet. Rats in one group were given all their calories in one meal and allowed only 30 minutes to eat. Rats in the other group could eat their calories all day.

Both groups of rats lost about the same amount of weight. The big difference came when the rats resumed normal eating. The rats that had eaten only one meal a day developed an increased ability to gain fat. After the experiment was over, they gained more weight than the rats who ate throughout the day.

So it's important that dieters eat several small meals throughout the day. Bodybuilders who prepare for competition by eating only one meal a day are making a mistake. They are setting themselves up for a big fat gain after the contest.

Whether or not I'm dieting, I eat three main meals plus a midafternoon snack and a bedtime snack. That's the best way to get lean and stay lean.

UPDATE:

Nutritionist Nancy Clark, writing in *Runners' World* magazine (March, 1984), described a study in which six people ate 2,000 calories in only one meal per day for a week. When they ate all the calories in the morning they lost two and a half pounds more than when they ate their one meal at night. This is consistent with the Cornell University finding that exercise after eating burns more calories than the same exercise done on an empty stomach. The subjects referred to by Nancy Clark burned more calories when they ate in the morning before their daily activity than when they ate at night and were inactive. So it also makes a difference when the one big meal is eaten.

On the other side of the "when to eat" question are the studies which show that exercising before you eat tends to depress the appetite and cause you to eat less. For example, a study found that food intake could be decreased in pre-school children by scheduling recess before rather than after lunch.

Pre-meal exercise also speeds up the metabolism so you burn more of the calories you eat. Additionally, exercise before eating, especially aerobic exercise, dissipates stress which may cause overeating.

All things considered, the best plan is to spread your meals throughout the day and avoid overeating when you're going to be inactive. You can't lose if you exercise daily—before or after meals—because you'll either eat less or burn more of the calories you do eat.

Understand The Problem With Desserts

Q. I do fine in my diet when I eat at home. My problem is I blow it when I eat out. I can't resist desserts. Any suggestions?

A. An occasional dessert never made anybody fat, but don't make it a habit. If you're going to have a dessert, a restaurant is the best place. There, you'll probably have only one dessert even though you might like to have more. At home it's too easy to have seconds or even thirds on desserts. At home the best rule on desserts is: Absolutely Not!

Understanding the problem with desserts will help you hold back in restaurants and also give you a handle on calorie control in general.

Desserts are filled with what I call "concentrated calories." Sugar and butter are good examples. Sugar and butter in particular, and concentrated calorie foods in general, have two key characteristics: 1) They contain no fiber and bulk. As a result, even a small amount of these foods will contain a large number of calories. 2) Concentrated calorie foods stimulate, rather than satisfy, your appetite.

Desserts make you fat because they contain a high concentration of calories. Even worse, they encourage you to eat more calories than you need or really want.

At the end of a good meal, at home or at a restaurant, I prefer a cup of coffee with cream and a little artificial sweetener. This satisfies me more than any gooey dessert. Avoid that first bite of concentrated calorie food, at home or out, and you'll have an important leg up on calorie control.

Splurge Occasionally

Q. My weakness is ice cream. I used to eat a quart at one sitting. I've replaced that with a low-calorie gelatin pudding made with nonfat milk. I eat two- to three-and-one-half cups a night with

Hunger and deprivation have no part in a diet for lifetime leanness. *Photo by Bill Reynolds.*

whipped topping. This usually satisfies my sweet tooth. Is this bad for me?

A. I think most people like ice cream. I know I do. When I really crave ice cream, I don't try to resist. I go to the ice-cream parlor and have a big sundae. The sundae goes down real easy and, when I finish, I'm usually tempted to have another, but I'm too embarrassed to order more. That's the beauty of eating dessert out instead of at home. "At home," as I said in my book *Ripped,* "it's too easy to have a second or even third helping of dessert."

As an alternative to having a low-calorie substitute every night, you might try going out and having the real thing occasionally. This takes the pressure off. You'll probably eat a reasonable amount and feel satisfied, and you'll be happy to go back to reasonable eating the next day. An occasional ice-cream splurge, eaten out, would probably be safer than your current nightly routine.

My view that it's helpful to satisfy your craving for ice cream and other fattening foods occasionally is shared by Nancy Clark, registered dietitian and author of the book *The Athlete's Kitchen.* Writing in the November, 1983 *Runner's World,* she says that we should "Keep in mind that only those who deny themselves their favorite foods respond to this denial by binge eating."

I'll see you at the ice cream parlor.

Go Ahead, Pig Out on Holidays

Q. Every once in a while, especially on holidays, I lose control and eat everything. I feel guilty afterwards. How can I keep from pigging out?

A. Don't. On holidays my mother-in-law usually invites my wife, my son and me to a big family dinner. She serves all of the things that Carol and I usually avoid: meat, gravy and dressing; she adds butter to everything; and never fixes less than three desserts. She loves to see me eat, and I don't disappoint her. I eat it all, including the three desserts. I take my time. I'm usually the last one to finish eating. I eat my fill of everything and I don't feel the least bit guilty. Then I'm happy to get back to my usual diet. In three or four days my weight is back to normal.

An occasional pig-out actually helps you stay on your diet. It completely satisfies your craving for fattening foods. This is important, because one of the keys to staying on a diet is to avoid feeling deprived. An occasional eating splurge won't make you fat. It's your regular eating pattern that really counts. Don't feel guilty. Enjoy it.

How To Keep It Off

Q. After losing 30 pounds, I look and feel better than I have in years, and I'm satisfied with my weight. My big fear is that I'll regain the weight I've lost and then some, as I have in the past. Do you have any suggestions to help me maintain my weight loss?

A. Statistics prove that your fear is fully justified. Only a small percentage, some say as low as five percent, of those who lose weight manage to keep it off. As Covert Bailey wrote in his book *Fit or Fat?*, "The American public has been dieting for 25 years—and has gained five pounds." I'll give you some methods that have helped me stay lean.

Weigh yourself every day, even after you overeat. This instant feedback helps you stay in control. It tells you which foods you can eat and which foods make you gain weight. Anytime your weight goes up a few pounds, tighten up on your diet until it's back down. I have a record of my morning weight going back years, and I plan to weigh myself every morning for the rest of my life. I suggest that you do the same.

Don't skip meals. People who go off in the morning without breakfast and have next to nothing for lunch are setting themselves up to eat everything in sight in the evening. You should eat on a regular schedule every day. Like daily weighing, this keeps you in control. Your blood sugar stays up, and you're not inclined to overeat at your next meal.

I eat three main meals, along with midafternoon and bedtime snacks. Apples are my favorite snack. My wife buys them by the 40-pound box. I don't know if it's true that "an apple a day keeps the doctor away," but I can tell you that apples are great for staying lean. When you know that circumstances are going to force you to miss a meal, I suggest that you take a few apples along to control your hunger until your next meal.

Eat whole, natural foods and avoid processed foods. Sybil Ferguson, the founder of The Diet Centers, suggests eating food in

I cut my peanut butter sandwich into six pieces to make it last longer. I also cut my carrot into small pieces. *Photo by Wayne Gallasch.*

"Mother Nature's wrapper." That's a good idea, because almost all processed foods have the fiber and bulk removed and sugar or fat added. The refining process almost always increases the calorie density of food and makes it more fattening than the natural version. So go easy on food that comes in a box, can, bottle or a package of any kind.

Plain, basic foods are best. Whole grains and fresh fruits and vegetables are Mother Nature's best stay-slim foods. They should make up a substantial part of your daily menu. By the same token, sauces and mixtures of various kinds are almost always fattening. To quote Sybil Ferguson again, "Keep it simple."

Finally, exercise regularly. Exercise burns extra calories and allows you to eat more without getting fat. In addition to your weight-training program do some type of aerobic exercise. Walking, biking, rowing, Heavyhands and rebounding are my favorites. I do one or more of these activities almost every day. Aerobic exercise three to five times a week will help you stay lean, but every day is better.

I won't kid you. Staying lean is a constant battle. But if you make up your mind that you want to live your life in a lean and attractive body, you can. Remember, you alone control what and how much you eat and how active you are. If you eat right and keep physically active, you'll stay lean.

CHAPTER FIVE

WEIGHT TRAINING BUILDS MUSCLE

CHAPTER FIVE: WEIGHT TRAINING BUILDS MUSCLE

Best Method

Q. For years the weight training gospel has been low reps and heavy weights for mass, and high reps with light weights for definition. Most bodybuilders still seem to follow this philosophy of training, but recently I've heard that some of the top men don't change their training routine; they rely mostly on diet to sharpen up for competition. Which method is best for getting ripped?

A. I've tried it both ways. Body composition tests proved that a combination of heavy weights, low (6-10) reps and an average of four sets per bodypart allowed me to lose more fat and retain more muscle. On a high rep and set routine, body composition tests showed that I lost more muscle than fat. During one six-week period in 1978 I used a high-rep and high-set routine, and my weight loss was 36 percent fat and 64 percent muscle.

I'm convinced that increasing reps and sets before a contest is a mistake. Maximum muscle is achieved by using heavy weights and low reps and sets. Minimum fat is achieved through a reduction in calories. Put the two together—heavy weights and low sets plus calorie reduction—and you have the formula for maximum muscle with minimum fat.

Reps For Thigh Cuts

Q. I have good definition in my upper body, but I'm having trouble getting cuts in my thighs. How many repetitions should I do to bring these out?

A. I'm repeatedly asked this question in one form or another. Doing reps is not the best way to achieve definition. Spot reducing doesn't work, either. To lose fat from one part of your body you have to lose it from all parts. Most of us have problem areas especially resistant to fat reduction. The hips and thighs are problem areas for some people; others have trouble with the abdominal area. The solution lies mainly in diet and aerobic exercise, not in high-repetition weight training.

Weight training is the best way to build and maintain muscle while you're losing fat, but it's not the best way to burn fat. Weight training is so intense that it can't be continued long enough to burn significant calories. I usually stick with 6-10 reps on most exercises, because that repetition range stimulates the maximum number of muscle fibers. Doing more reps doesn't burn substantially more fat. All it does is tire you out and reduce the intensity of the exercise.

Walking comes about as close as anything to being a pure fat-burning activity. This is because it can be continued for a long period of time without developing an oxygen debt. Oxygen is required to burn body fat. When exercise becomes so intense that you cannot meet the demand for oxygen, you stop burning fat and rely on stored carbohydrate (glycogen) in the muscles for energy. In his excellent book *Fit or Fat?*, Covert Bailey makes a dramatic comment on walking I'll never forget. He says, "If I were grossly fat, I would give up whatever was necessary—job, housework, whatever—and I would walk three or four hours per day." I don't go quite that far, but when I'm trying to achieve maximum leanness I often walk and/or bike as much as two hours a day.

I suggest that you stick with the number of repetitions best for building and maintaining muscle mass—6-10 reps with the heaviest weights you can handle in good form. Then use aerobic exercise combined with a balanced low-calorie diet to reduce your overall level of body fat until you achieve the desired degree of definition in your thighs.

Fast Or Slow Reps?

Q. Two famous bodybuilders recently gave seminars at the gym where I train. One recommended fast reps to burn more fat. He demonstrated by driving his Presses up so fast the plates rattled. Later, when I asked the other champ about this to make sure I had it straight, he told me to do my exercises in a slow and controlled manner. I'm confused. Can you help me?

A. I can understand your problem. To succeed at bodybuilding you have to sift through a lot of conflicting information and decide for yourself what makes sense and what's best for you.

A fast style of exercise may be desirable at times. An example would be training to improve your performance in a sport that requires fast, explosive movements. A shot-putter would benefit from fast, explosive presses. Fast reps, however, won't help you burn more fat. Fat is burned out of your muscles when your energy output exceeds your caloric intake, and fast reps won't speed up the process.

Generally, doing your exercises in a slow controlled style is best for overall muscle development. This is particularly important when you're reducing, because the muscle tissue that's being used will be maintained while fat is burned away. Muscle tissue not being used because of incorrect exercise performance is likely to be lost along with the fat. Strive to use every muscle fiber to keep from losing it while you're reducing your body fat.

In order to maintain every muscle fiber, you must do your exercises in a manner that causes every part of the muscle to contract. To do this, you must perform each repetition slowly, insuring that the weight is moved through the full range of motion by muscular action alone. If you use a fast style, the weight will be moved through the range of motion partly by momentum. In effect, the weight is thrown up rather than lifted. The muscle works only at the beginning to get the weight into motion. Momentum, not muscle, is used to complete the repetition. If you jerk or throw the weight up, you'll be working only part of the muscle.

My own experiments have shown that it's difficult to maintain muscle tissue while losing fat. What it comes down to is: Use it or lose it.

Calf Muscles Are No Exception

Q. I've read that the calves are made up of high-endurance, slow-twitch muscle fibers and therefore need high reps to grow. Is that true?

A. No. The gastrocnemius, the most prominent part of the calf, is made up mostly of fast-twitch muscle fibers. The underlying soleus is predominantly slow-twitch, but has some fast-twitch fibers.

Read my discussion of fast- and slow-twitch muscle fibers in

Calves should be trained hard, heavy and infrequently. Don't waste time with light weights and high reps. *Photo by Bill Reynolds.*

Photo by Bill Reynolds.

Chapter Eight. First, slow-twitch fibers won't grow bigger to any appreciable degree and, second, it takes heavy, slow movements to make fast-twitch muscle fibers grow. When you do high repetitions (20-25) you're simply wearing yourself out with low-force movements. It's the last few repetitions of a set that are the high-intensity reps, the ones that make the muscle grow. If you do 20 or more repetitions before you get to the high-intensity reps, you'll be too tired to do the last few with maximum intensity. Therefore, it's better to use a heavier weight and fewer repetitions (6-10).

The calves are tough muscles. What they need to make them grow is full, heavy, slow movements. Hit your calves hard, heavy and briefly; don't waste your time with light weights and high reps.

Focus On Progression

Q. I was very interested in the "Coaxing Long-Term Gains" excerpt from your book *Ripped 2,* which recently appeared in *Muscle & Fitness* where, as I understood it, you said you had made good gains by stopping your sets just short of failure. I've always been afraid to try that, because I wasn't sure I'd be stimulating muscular growth. I'd be concerned that I wasn't training hard enough.

I've pored over articles and books trying to find reliable research on the intensity required to stimulate muscular growth, but I've never been able to find solid support for my feeling that less might be better. Do you know of any physiology text or research papers that would put my mind to rest on this point?

A. I think you'd find *Physiology of Exercise* (Wm. C. Brown Company Publishers, Third Edition, 1980) by Herbert A. deVries helpful. You'll find this book in most university bookstores or libraries. It's often used in undergraduate and graduate-level courses in exercise physiology. I keep a copy in my office and frequently refer to it.

Until shortly after World War II, most physical educators and researchers believed that weight training would limit an athlete's range of motion and speed—that is, make him musclebound. Consequently, little research was done on strength training. After World War II, there was a great need for scientific evaluation of weight-training procedures to aid in rehabilitation of injured veterans. According to Dr. deVries, this new interest in strength training soon laid the musclebound myth to rest and produced a substantial amount of research into the best way to stimulate muscle growth.

Here's a brief summary, based on Dr. deVries' text, of what research has revealed about the best way to train for gains in size and strength:

1) Overload makes a muscle bigger and stronger. Overload occurs when a muscle works against substantially greater resistance than that to which it's accustomed.

2) Maximal contraction produces the fastest gains, but the threshold level at which strength and size gains begin to appear is 35 percent of maximum.

3) If less than maximum contraction is used, it should be used on a continuing re-evaluation of what constitutes maximum. The resistance must be increased as the maximum strength level increases.

4) All contractions should be made through a full range of motion. That's because strength gains are specific to the angle at which resistance is applied.

5) For the development of strength, two or three sets of 4-10 repetitions each, using maximum resistance for the number of repetitions, has been experimentally proven effective.

6) For the development of muscle size, the DeLorme technique below is probably most effective:

1 set of 10 repetitions with 50 percent of 10-repetition maximum.
1 set of 10 repetitions with 75 percent of 10-repetition maximum.
1 set of 10 repetitions with 100 percent of 10-repetition maximum.

7) Workouts should probably be scheduled three to five times a week, depending on your other vigorous activities.

8) Probably no more than one workout per week should approach exhaustion.

What it comes down to is that muscles grow in size and strength when they're continually forced to work harder than they're used to working. That's why I focus on progression. I continually try to lift a few more pounds or do a few more repetitions than I've done before. This doesn't necessarily mean pushing to the absolute limit, however. In fact, as Dr. deVries says, it's not a good idea to push to exhaustion, or failure, more often than once a week; and even then, I think it's a good idea to save a little for the next heavy workout.

Overload makes a muscle bigger and stronger. *Photo by Denie.*

Psychologically, I don't like to fail. Stopping just short of my limit and increasing the weight in small increments gives me confidence for my next workout. I've found that I make my best long-term gains when I lift a little more each heavy workout but don't try to squeeze out every possible repetition.

According to Dr. deVries, research indicates that maximal contractions give the fastest results, but contractions less than maximal also produce results. It's important to note that Dr. deVries also says that an untrained individual gains faster than someone who has been training a long time. I suspect that always pushing to the limit may work better for a beginning bodybuilder than for someone more advanced. In part, this is because most beginners haven't learned how to contract their muscles maximally; therefore, they can benefit from pushing to their perceived limit more often than can an advanced bodybuilder.

Additionally, an advanced bodybuilder shouldn't expect to gain in size and strength throughout the full course of the year. I spend approximately three months of the year using light weights and doing many sets and exercises. I rarely push to my limit during this period. For another six months I do fewer exercises and sets, and use heavier weights. I use moderate intensity during this period and usually stop a rep or two short of my absolute limit.

The only time I train to failure or very close to failure is the last three months of the year when I'm peaking. During this period my workouts are short and heavy. But even during my peaking period I usually don't train to failure more often than once a week.

During 1983, I achieved my lifetime best results by training as I've just described. I made it a point to lift a little more weight or do another repetition or two each heavy workout. I increased the weight continuously, but not enough to stall my progress. This allowed me to keep making gains throughout my three-month peaking period. I believe this moderate approach allowed me to gain more muscle and lose more fat than ever before. My body composition changes leading up to and during my 1983 peaking period are shown on the accompanying graph. You can see that I accomplished what every bodybuilder wants: I simultaneously lost fat (9.09 pounds) and gained muscle (10.84 pounds).

I believe you're correct that less is often better. Whether you train to failure or save a little for the next workout, as I usually do, remember that the key to muscular gains is progression. You must

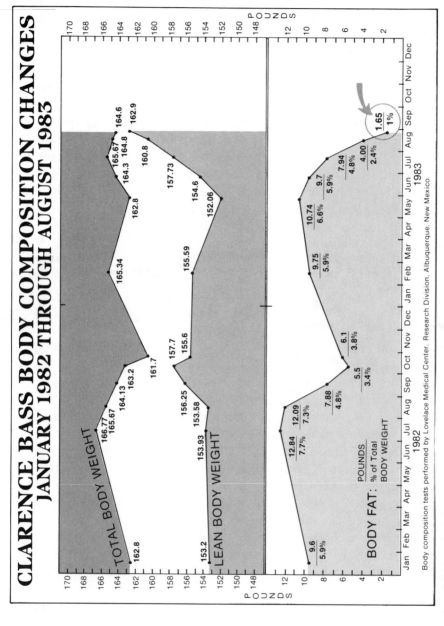

CLARENCE BASS BODY COMPOSITION CHANGES
JANUARY 1982 THROUGH AUGUST 1983

Body composition tests performed by Lovelace Medical Center, Research Division, Albuquerque, New Mexico.

In October of 1982, my body fat climbed .4 percent despite a drop in bodyweight. The reason: Dieting too strictly caused body fat rebound. I didn't make the same mistake in 1983; my muscle mass continued to climb while my body fat went down to one percent. *Graph by Typography Unlimited.*

overload your muscles by forcing them to work against greater and greater resistance.

The Problem With Training To Failure

Q. What is your opinion on training to failure?

A. I'm convinced that training to failure is the best way to stimulate muscle growth. The problem is that it's hard to face up to this type of training workout after workout.

Arthur Jones, inventor of the Nautilus machines, wrote in *Nautilus Training Principles, Bulletin No. 1,* "A set should be terminated only when it is impossible to move the weight in any position, when the bar literally drops out of your exhausted hands." Jones realizes, however, that the biggest problem with this type of training is motivation. It's virtually impossible for an individual to push to a 100 percent effort consistently.

Albert Beckles, 1982 and 1984 World Professional Bodybuilding Champion, recently put his finger on the problem with training to total failure. He said, "I personally think that if you 'freak' yourself out too much on an exercise then you don't feel like training anymore." Simply put, it's no fun to train that way, and if you try to train to failure all the time, your body and your mind eventually rebel.

As I see it, the problem is to derive the physiological benefits of training to failure and still maintain the desire to train. I'll tell you some techniques I use to maintain my motivation.

At times in the past I've tried to train continuously with maximum intensity, but I learned that it's mentally and physically impossible. Now, I train really hard for only three or four months each year. The rest of the year I train with less intensity, concentrating on general conditioning or taking medium-volume workouts. This is the way top athletes in most sports train. They build themselves up each year for a big push. This keeps them mentally and physically fresh and allows them to reach a higher level of performance each year. This is both the most enjoyable and most effective way to train.

Even when I'm making my big push each year I still don't train with maximum intensity every workout. I've found that I make my best gains if I follow my heavy training sessions with light or medium workouts. By training heavily intermittently, three or four times a month, I'm able to stay enthusiastic about working out and continually push myself to lift heavier and heavier weights.

Finally, I focus my training on progression, on continually lifting another pound or two or doing a few more reps. Only rarely do I push myself to gut-busting failure; it's not necessary. What is necessary is to train hard enough to keep making gains. It's a fine line to walk—lifting more than before but just short of failure. I'm convinced, however, that it's the best way to keep gaining year after year.

Sticking Points

Q. I began training with weights twice in my life. Once in my 20s, and again in my early 30s. Both times I made great gains for seven-nine months. Then I hit a sticking point and I was unable to make any gains whatsoever. I tried taking a week off and changing my routine. It didn't help. Both times I gave up in frustration.

I'm contemplating starting bodybuilding again but this time I would like to have a plan for overcoming my sticking point when it occurs. What strategy should I use when I reach a sticking point again?

A. Your question comes at an appropriate time. I'm now in the final stages of my peaking program for 1981, and I think I have handled it better this year than ever before. My lifts are at an all-time high. For example, in 1979, I peaked in the Leg Press at 650 pounds times 15 repetitions. In 1980, I peaked at 700 pounds times 10 reps. This year I've already done 700 pounds times 15 reps and 750 pounds times 10 reps. Over the years I've fought my way through many sticking points, and I have developed some strategies which allow me to keep gaining year after year.

First, bodybuilding gains, like gains in any other activity, are sporadic. Every athlete experiences peaks, valleys and plateaus. You can't expect to make continuous, steady progress with no setbacks. Almost anybody would peak out after gaining for seven-nine months as you did.

I plan my routines on a yearly basis. Most bodybuilders and other athletes do the same. You should take a similar long-term approach. You might try training hard each year for six-nine months and then backing off to give your body a chance to recuperate. During the other three-six months of the year you should go on a maintenance routine, training with medium to light weights and emphasizing aerobic exercises such as running, cycling, handball, or whatever appeals to you. This type of cyclical training program will enable you to keep gaining year after year.

This year I made it a point to coax, rather than force, my body to continually handle heavier and heavier weights. For example, in 1980, I set my sights on lifting 700 pounds times 15 reps in the Leg Press. I pushed as hard as I could in every workout and I sometimes increased my Leg Press by as much as 25 pounds from one workout to the next. I think my rush to 700 pounds was what made me peak at 10 reps with that weight rather than going up to 15 reps, which was my goal.

I held back this year and only increased my poundages 10 pounds at a time, even though I often felt I could progress faster. This gave me confidence for my next workout. I knew I could lift more each workout because I had quit a little short of my limit the previous workout. This coaxing rather than forcing worked well for me. I suggest that you try a similar strategy. Both your head and your body will be willing to go farther if you stop a little short of your absolute limit in each workout.

I used another technique this year which is similar to the coaxing technique I've just described. I train on a four-day cycle, taking three days to work my whole body and then resting on the fourth day. I alternate heavy cycles with what I call "regular cycles." On one cycle I use heavy weights for six-eight reps, plus I use forced reps, negatives and the rest/pause technique. On the next cycle I back off a little and use less weight (about 80 percent), increasing my reps to the 8-12 range. During this cycle I do no forced, negative or rest/pause sets. Alternating heavy and regular cycles kept me progressing. It gave my body and mind a reprieve every other cycle. You should try this technique.

It's also important that you listen to your body. There will be times when you have not recovered sufficiently to blast into your next workout. On these days, reduce your training or substitute a walk or a bike ride for your weight training workout. Be flexible and you'll keep gaining.

Short- and long-term goals are extremely important. Pick a goal each year, such as a contest, a picture-taking session, a body fat percentage, or whatever motivates you. Work to achieve that goal, and once you do, back off for a while and set another long-term goal. You should also have short-term goals on a workout-to-workout basis. A training diary will help you establish short-term goals. After each heavy workout I write down in my training diary, based on how that workout went, what I plan to do in my next heavy cycle. Try this. It'll keep you gaining.

If you expect ups and downs in your training, you'll be less likely to be frustrated by them when they occur. Bodybuilding is a lifetime pursuit. Plan to keep training forever. Be flexible, intelligent and, above all, patient. Don't try to blast through sticking points. When you come to a brick wall, back up, then plan a way to get around the wall.

The Importance of Change

Q. How often should I change my training routine? How often do you change yours?

A. Dr. Tom McLaughlin of the National Strength Research Center at Auburn University says, I think correctly: "No fixed workout, no matter how perfect, will work for very long. Any training program that does not effectively and systematically utilize change will eventually lead to overtraining and lack of progress." The body quickly becomes accustomed to a routine, and when this happens, gains stop coming. A change of routine shocks the body into further adaptation and gains resume. Joe Weider calls this the Muscle Confusion Principle. If you use change properly, your muscles never have a chance to fully adjust; they stay confused and keep trying to adapt by getting stronger.

I continually change my training program. When I stop seeing gains from an exercise, usually after four or five weeks, I change the exercise. It doesn't take much of a change to alter the effect significantly. Often a change of hand spacing or body position is enough. For example, I recently moved from a narrow grip to a wide grip on Barbell Bent Rows and noticed an immediate response. My lats became sore and stiff, and my enthusiasm for the exercise immediately returned. I experienced the same positive reaction when I changed from a kneeling to a standing position on the Dumbbell Kickback exercise for triceps. Changing from barbell to

86

It's important to vary your training program and work your muscles from many different angles.
Photo by Wayne Gallasch.

dumbbells is another simple way to trigger a further adaptive response. Of course, changing to a completely different exercise also does the job.

There is no set rule for how often you should change exercises. Beginners don't need to change as often as advanced bodybuilders. Pay careful attention to how your muscles respond to a particular exercise. As soon as you start struggling and are no longer able to increase the weight, it's time to change. It may be three months or more before a beginner plateaus, while gains may stop coming for an experienced bodybuilder in as little as two or three weeks.

When you do change, start with a weight that you can handle comfortably. This gives you time to work back up to your previous level, and then go higher.

I also find that it helps to vary intensity. If I'm training my body twice a week, I can avoid staleness longer by training heavy once and light or medium the other time. For instance, if my maximum is 10 repetitions with 100 pounds, I train my body at that level once a week and then back off to 10 repetitions with 85 pounds for the second training cycle that week.

I also change the volume and intensity of my training over the course of a year. For about three months I do a lot of volume but keep the intensity low, training each body part from many different angles, but I don't use a lot of weight. For the next six months, I do fewer exercises and increase the intensity. For the final three months, I use low volume and high intensity; I do only a few exercises for each body part, but I use as much weight as I can in good form. Changing like this lets me keep improving. Each year my peak is higher.

Change is very important in my training program. Make it a regular part of your routine as well. McLaughlin summed it up in *Powerlifting-USA* magazine: "Whether you change the way you do an exercise by altering stance, grip, bar placement, the movement itself, speed of the motion, or periodically use a different exercise altogether, the key is to change."

Too Much Warm-Up

Q. I'm getting back into bodybuilding after a layoff. As a general warm-up I plan to jog in place for one minute, do 10 free Squats, 10

Push-Ups and 10 Chin-Ups. As my condition improves I plan to increase my general warm-up to jogging in place for four minutes, and doing three sets of 20 free Squats, three sets of 20 Push-Ups and three sets of 20 Chin-Ups. What do you think of my plan?

A. A warm-up is necessary for optimal muscle performance, but it shouldn't be overdone.

During my Olympic lifting days I competed against a medical doctor who didn't believe in warming up. I can remember he would come into the gym, load the bar to a near maximum snatch poundage, concentrate briefly and make a beautiful lift—with absolutely no warm-up. I saw him do this repeatedly.

It seemed to work well for him, but my body always told me that some warm-up was necessary. However, my exposure to this doctor did convince me that excessive warm-up is a waste of time. It's also counterproductive. If you wear yourself out warming up, you can't do justice to your heavy sets.

Certainly, warming up helps physically and mentally. It puts you in the mood to work out and prepares you psychologically for maximum effort. It's also a safeguard against injury. A warm-up increases the elasticity of the tendons and ligaments, and causes a rise in the temperature of the muscle cells, which speeds up the production of energy. A cold muscle simply can't perform up to its capacity.

So a general warm-up is a good idea. There is no need, however, to do progressively more warming up as your condition improves. Only do enough to get your blood flowing. A few minutes of easy exercise on a stationary bicycle or a mini-trampoline is a good general warm-up. I don't like jogging in place; it's murder on cold joints.

I usually start out by doing a few Arm Swings, Toe Touches and Deep Knee Bends. After that I warm up for each specific exercise. For large muscle groups (e.g. back and legs), I generally do two or three warm-up sets. For smaller muscle groups (e.g. shoulders and arms), I find that one or two warm-up sets is adequate. I use a weight considerably below the weight I plan to use for my maximum set or sets and I do only enough to get the particular muscles warmed up for the heavy set or sets.

For example, in the Leg Press, I usually do two or three warm-up sets. On these sets I use successively heavier weights and restrict myself to five or six repetitions. These repetitions are just enough to warm up the areas involved, but not enough to tire the muscles and detract from the effort and intensity I can put into the heaviest set or sets. In an exercise like the Curl, I do only one warm-up set with a medium weight and then go immediately to my heaviest set.

The most important advice I can give you on warming up is this: warm up, certainly, but don't waste precious energy and recovery capacity on unnecessary and nonproductive warm-up exercises. Save your energy for the sets that count—the heavy sets.

Rest Interval

Q. How long do you recommend that a bodybuilder rest between sets?

A. It depends on your goal. If you're trying to increase your cardiorespiratory fitness as well as your muscular development, you should keep the rest interval between sets short. To increase your cardiorespiratory fitness you must keep your heart and breathing rate elevated for at least 15 minutes—and preferably longer. This means you shouldn't allow your breathing and heart rate to return to normal between sets, but should rest briefly (15-30 seconds), and then continue. This, however, is not the best way to build muscle mass and strength.

As a contest approaches, I allow myself to recover fully between sets so I can put maximum intensity into each set. This is important when your goal is to lose fat and become more muscular. It's difficult to lose fat without losing muscle, but training helps you keep your muscle. Muscle fibers that are being used are likely to be retained while body fat is lost; muscle fibers that aren't being used are likely to be lost. To insure the use of every muscle fiber possible, you must maintain the highest training intensity you can. This can best be accomplished by allowing full recovery between sets and putting maximum effort, unhampered by breathlessness, into each set.

The need for greater intensity as competition approaches is something that bodybuilders and runners have in common. Grete Waitz, the champion marathon runner from Norway, described her speed training in *The Runner* magazine. In the winter she uses interval training with very short recovery periods. For instance, she runs 220 yards at a fast pace 15 or 20 times with 20-second rest intervals. But in the spring, as competition gets closer, she switches from interval training to repetition training, in which she takes a full recovery between each run. This allows her to run harder and faster. The end result, for Grete, is greater muscular strength and faster times in competition. For the bodybuilder, longer rest periods and heavier, more intense workouts mean maximum muscle and minimum fat at contest time.

There is no set time for the rest period between sets. I recommend that you rest until your breathing returns to normal. Listen to your body and it will tell you when you are ready, physically and mentally, to put maximum intensity into your next set. Try to strike a balance. Don't rest so long that you cool off, but don't start up again before you're recovered. On an average I rest from 1-3 minutes between sets—one minute for smaller muscle groups like arms and shoulders, closer to three minutes for large muscle groups like back and legs.

If your goal is to get ripped, rest between sets until you're recovered enough to put in maximum effort again.

No Energy

Q. I've been training with weights for two years. I use a high-intensity split routine. I train Monday, Wednesday, Friday and Saturday, and my workouts last about two hours. On Sunday I ride a bicycle 15-20 miles. My problem is I look fit, but I feel run-down. I eat a well-balanced diet with plenty of carbohydrates. But at work the fat guys have more energy than I do. Can you help me?

A. Getting ripped doesn't require that you tolerate that run-down feeling. I've brought my body fat below three percent repeatedly without experiencing fatigue. You should feel good while you're getting ripped. If you don't, there's something wrong with your diet or training.

In bodybuilding, a low-carbohydrate diet can cause lack of energy. However, we can eliminate a low-carb diet as the cause of your problem because you say you eat a balanced diet.

It sounds like you're overtraining and not allowing yourself enough recovery time between workouts. You have only so much energy and you must use it carefully. The amount of stress and the time allowed for recovery are critical to the success of any training program.

I note the length of each workout in my training diary; I try to limit each session to about one hour. *Photo by Wayne Gallasch.*

Two hours is too long for a high-intensity workout. Short, quality workouts are best. For instance, I limit my workouts to one hour or less. I rarely do more than four all-out sets per bodypart. I maintain a steady workout pace, but I'm careful to rest enough between sets to insure I am fully recovered and ready for the next set. Workout pace and duration are keys to productive training.

In February of 1981, track star Don Paige set an indoor world record in the 1000-meter run. *Sports Illustrated* reported that two weeks before the race Paige strained the tendon on the inside of his left ankle. Consequently, he did not train the week before his record-breaking run. "I've rested totally," he said. "I haven't jogged a step." Paige's performance underlines the importance of rest in a training program.

I suggest that you cut your workouts back to one hour or less and make sure that you recover from your Sunday bike rides before your Monday training sessions. A good first step would be for you to follow Don Paige's example and "rest totally" for a week. Remember, training intensity is important, but rest is equally important.

Signs of Overtraining

Q. How can I tell when I'm overtraining?

A. The classic signs of overtraining are restless sleep, loss of appetite, reduced performance and elevated resting heart rate. At its most severe, overtraining can bring on exhaustion, illness and even collapse. It's important for you to be able to detect the first subtle signs of overtraining.

In his book *The Running Revolution* (Gemini Books, 1980), Joe Henderson includes a quote from Dr. Tom Bassler, which in my experience is right on the money: "The first thing that goes when you start to work too hard is your sense of humor. You get bitchy. You take yourself too seriously. You think inconvenience is a catastrophe."

That's how it is with me. The first thing I notice when I train too much, too hard or too often is that I become irritable. Things that ordinarily wouldn't bother me get on my nerves. I don't have any patience. To borrow from one of Joe Henderson's correspondents, Amy Wachtler, I add an MD after my name—Miserable

Disposition, that is.

At the more obvious level, my joints begin to ache, and I can't go to sleep at night even though I'm tired. When I do manage to go to sleep, I wake up several times during the night feeling very restless. When I try to train, my muscles feel flat; they don't respond to exercise the way they usually do. My workouts become a chore.

Every enthusiastic bodybuilder encounters overtraining from time to time. You'll get better results from your training, and those around you will like you more, if you learn to recognize the signs of overtraining, especially the first subtle signs—irritability, no sense of humor and no patience.

Muscular Soreness as a Training Aid

Q. I use soreness to gauge the effectiveness of my workouts. After each workout I rate my soreness on a scale of 1-10 and record it in my training diary. What are your thoughts on muscular soreness?

A. The precise physiological causes of muscular soreness aren't completely understood, but there's no question that careful observation of soreness can help you in several ways. I'm not referring to crippling soreness that can force a layoff of a week or more and retard training progress. This can be avoided by proper warm-up and by gradually accustoming your body to heavy training. The soreness that can be helpful is more of a stiffness in your muscles.

First, slight soreness or a "used" feeling in my muscles tells me that I had a good workout. It means that I pushed my body a little farther than before and that I can expect compensation in the form of increased strength and muscle. I welcome this type of soreness as a measure of training intensity.

Soreness is also valuable in determining the effect of a particular exercise. When I try a new exercise I'm careful to observe the resulting soreness because it tells me what muscle or muscles I've worked. When I'm sore I always try to determine what exercise or activity caused the soreness. This helps me evaluate particular exercises and plan future workouts.

By all means continue to record your soreness. You should also note how long your soreness lasts because it will help you determine whether you're recovering between training sessions.

You'll also be interested in my discussion of the cause of muscular soreness in Chapter Eight.

Recovery Training

Q. In my eagerness to reach a reasonable standard of development, I have grossly overtrained. I have been training for five years. Because my upper body development was lagging, I trained my upper body far more often and with far more sets than my legs. To my great surprise, my legs have grown and my upper body hasn't. I believe I did not allow my upper body enough time to recover between workouts. How important is the recuperation time between workouts, and what is the best way to speed recovery?

A. Some authorities say the body will adapt to any stress if given enough time. In support of this theory, they cite the Russian and Bulgarian Olympic weightlifters who are said to train daily, lifting near maximum poundages. I don't really know how the Russian and Bulgarian lifters train, but I'm sure that overtraining is a common bodybuilding mistake.

Bodybuilders could learn from runners who do a lot of "recovery" runs. Arthur Lydiard, the famous running coach from New Zealand, advocates gentle aerobic runs to assist in the recovery from anaerobic training. Many long distance running coaches say that you should never do two hard workouts in succession. Every hard run should be followed by at least one easy run.

Craig Virgin, former world cross-country champion and second-place finisher in the 1980 Boston Marathon, prepared for the Boston race by following each hard run with one or two easy, recovery runs.

Last year I incorporated recovery training into my bodybuilding workouts and made better progress than ever before. I did this in two ways: 1) I used a four-day cycle, taking three days to hit all bodyparts and then resting on the fourth day. I followed each heavy cycle with a recovery cycle of medium to light training. 2) In addition, I took a cue from Arthur Lydiard and followed every weight-training session with a walk of about 20 minutes. The gentle aerobic stimulation of walking after each workout seemed to reduce my muscle soreness and stiffness. Walking increased my pulse rate, helping my muscles unload waste products faster and thereby speeding my recovery. The walks also speeded up my metabolism and allowed me to burn more calories.

I'm convinced that recuperation, active and passive, is more important than many bodybuilders realize.

Training With Injuries

Q. I injured my elbow so I can't do curls or work my lats without pain. I don't want to injure myself further, but I don't want to stop training my biceps and back either. What should I do?

A. A good rule to follow when you have an injury is "If it hurts, don't do it." If it really hurts, see your doctor immediately so he can help you get rid of the acute pain and speed up healing.

You can usually find a way to train around an injury and continue making progress while it heals. I've had to cope with a number of injuries during my almost 30 years of training, and I usually find a way to keep training in spite of the injury. I like heavy Squats, but occasionally they irritate my lower back. When this happens, I can still work my thighs very effectively if I stick to exercises where my back is stabilized, like Leg Presses, Hack Squats and Leg Extensions. I also have a shoulder problem that sometimes keeps me from doing Presses. I have nevertheless continued to make gains in my shoulders and chest. When this problem arises, I train my shoulders with a variety of Rowing motions and use the Crossover Pulley and Pec Deck for my chest.

Regarding your elbow injury, you can probably find a way to continue training your upper back and possibly your biceps without hurting your elbow. A number of machines—the Nautilus pullover is one—allow you to train your back without involving your biceps or your elbows. It's going to be harder to work your biceps without pain. Using a cambered curling bar, an E-Z curl bar, might take the strain off your elbow. Experiment and see if you can find a curling motion that doesn't hurt.

If your elbow hurts no matter what you do, then continue training your other parts and use rest and physical therapy on your elbow until the injury heals. Usually, however, if you're innovative, you can find a way to keep training the affected body part in spite of the injury.

96

When shoulder problems prevented me from doing presses, I trained my deltoids with Upright Rows and used the Crossover Pulley and Pec Deck for my chest. *Photos by Denie.*

The Pec Deck allowed me to work my chest without hurting my shoulder. *Photo by Bill Reynolds.*

Home vs. Gym Training

Q. There are no bodybuilding gyms where I live, so I have to train at home by myself. Can I make the same gains doing this as I could if I trained at a gym?

A. I've trained seriously for close to 30 years, and almost all my training has been at home. I taught myself the Olympic lifts by studying pictures and reading articles in the various muscle magazines. I became a national-caliber Olympic lifter while training at home without a coach. I succeeded at bodybuilding the same way. No doubt about it, you can make terrific progress training at home alone.

A simple yes, however, doesn't do justice to your question. Training experience and temperament have a lot to do with whether you will make good gains at home.

If you're just getting into bodybuilding, I suggest that, first, you study the training articles in *Muscle & Fitness* magazine. Then I suggest you arrange to do some workouts at a gym where a qualified instructor can prepare a beginner's program for you and teach you how to perform the basic exercises properly.

In his article on calf training in the June, 1980, issue of *Muscle & Fitness,* Chris Dickerson revealed that he did his very first workout under the guidance of Bill Pearl. I'm sure Chris avoided many mistakes by seeking good advice when he decided to start weight training.

Locate the bodybuilding gym in the city nearest your home, and go there for some help with your initial workouts. This way you can go home confident that you know what you're doing and that you'll make good progress right from the start. When you get further along and have more questions, return to the gym for a few more supervised workouts.

Many of the champs also offer personalized advice by mail for a fee. If you're not fully satisfied with the instruction that you receive at the gym, pick out the expert you think is most likely to be able to help you and drop him or her a line, explaining your problem.

Very experienced bodybuilders can often make better progress training at home than at a gym. Before he won the 1976 Mr. Olympia, Franco Columbu trained at home. Frank Zane does some of his most intense training in his own gym. If you're properly motivated and know what you're doing, you can concentrate better

Most of my training is at home, but I occasionally go to a commercial gym. These photos were taken at Gold's Gym in Santa Monica, right after I won my class in the 1978 Past-40 Mr. America. *Photos by Denie.*

and get more from your workouts at home, where you aren't bothered by the distractions present in any commercial gym.

I prefer training at home most of the time, but the occasional workout I do at a gym always gives me new ideas and renewed enthusiasm. Training at places like Gold's or some other center of bodybuilding activity is bound to give you new ideas and stimulate your training drive.

Some people do have a hard time keeping up their motivation when they train alone. If you have this problem, I'll bet you can find a friend who'll be willing to train with you, at least occasionally. I'd recommend, however, that you don't become too dependent on a training partner. If you do, you'll be in for a big letdown when your partner cancels out on you at the last minute.

But to repeat, if you approach it intelligently, you can succeed by training at home, and in some cases you may be able to do better at home than at a gym.

CHAPTER SIX

AEROBIC EXERCISE BURNS FAT

Good Chapter

CHAPTER SIX: AEROBIC EXERCISE BURNS FAT

Running For Definition

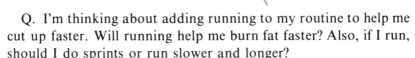

Read

Q. I'm thinking about adding running to my routine to help me cut up faster. Will running help me burn fat faster? Also, if I run, should I do sprints or run slower and longer?

A. Some bodybuilders do run before a contest for added definition. I don't. It's best to rely mostly on diet to get ripped and save all of your energy and drive for your workouts. You must keep your training intensity as high as possible to retain muscle tissue while burning off fat. If you're tired from running, it will be practically impossible for you to train heavy enough and hard enough to maintain muscle size.

Running will help you burn more calories. If you do decide to run, then slower, longer runs are better than sprints for burning body fat. If you do sprints, your body will require quick energy, and quick energy comes from the glycogen stored in your muscles and from fast-burning carbohydrate foods. If you run at a slower pace, your body can meet its energy needs by burning body fat, which supplies energy at a slower rate.

A good rule to follow is to keep your pace slow enough to allow you to carry on a conversation with a running companion. A "conversational pace" will allow you to burn mostly body fat and will allow you to run longer comfortably and, therefore, burn more calories.

Slow running is also less fatiguing and will leave you with more energy and drive for your weight workouts. To burn a few more calories and lose fat faster before a contest, but still keep my energy level high, I sometimes add fast walking. But I would never add sprints.

In the off-season I bicycle fast and long for cardiovascular fitness. I usually ride for about an hour, covering 20 miles. Endurance training—bicycling, running, racquetball, et cetera—is important. I recommend it to round out a total fitness program, particularly if you're over 30.

UPDATE:

In April of 1980, when I wrote the column in which this question appeared, I wasn't using aerobic exercise during the peaking phase of my training. As the answers that follow indicate, I've changed my approach. Aerobic exercise—walking, biking, rowing, Heavyhands and rebounding—is now a very important part of my training regimen, year-round. One of the truly exciting and stimulating aspects of my training and writing is continuing to learn and develop. I have been training for over 30 years, and I still learn something new almost every day.

Bodybuilding & Cardiovascular Fitness

Q. I just finished reading an article in the May, 1980, issue of *The Runner* magazine entitled "Weights Don't Work." The article raised a question in my mind. How effective is weight work for cardiovascular fitness? Jogging bores me, and I think most marathon runners look like concentration camp inmates. I'd like to develop some muscle, but I'm also interested in fitness.

A. Running is one of the best ways to develop cardiovascular fitness, but I agree with you that it doesn't develop the kind of physique admired by most *Muscle & Fitness* readers.

Many fitness experts maintain that weight training doesn't improve cardiovascular condition. If most of your time in the gym is spent sitting on the equipment rather than using it, they're correct. If, on the other hand, you follow the Weider Quality Training Principle, resting only 10-15 seconds between sets so your heart rate is kept at a high level throughout the workout, then weight training will develop cardiovascular fitness.

Mike Katz—Mr. America, Mr. World, and a Mr. Olympia contender—had his oxygen uptake capacity measured in an exercise physiology laboratory. Oxygen uptake capacity (the capability of the body to use oxygen) is the best measure of cardiovascular fitness. Katz amazed the researchers by demonstrating an extremely high oxygen uptake capacity.

In July of 1977, I myself had my oxygen uptake capacity

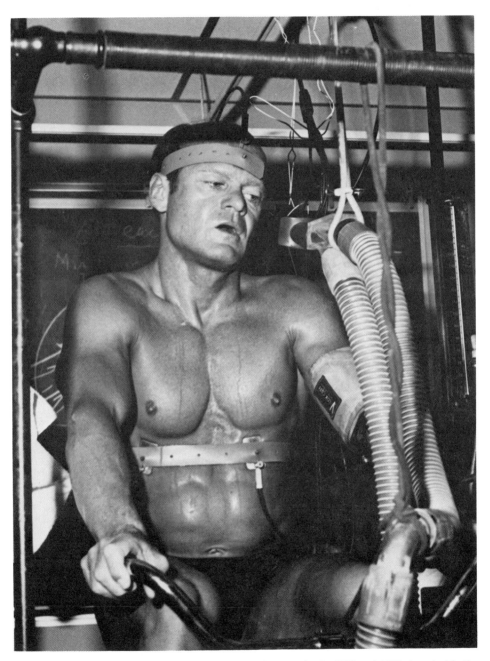

Lovelace Medical Center measured my oxygen uptake capacity in 1977 and 1981. I ranked in the excellent category both times, but I did slightly better in 1981—55 percent above average versus 50 percent. *Photo by Bill Reynolds.*

measured at Albuquerque's Lovelace Medical Center. The doctors at Lovelace had also heard that bodybuilding didn't develop cardiovascular fitness and they were surprised to find my oxygen uptake capacity 50 percent above average. My cardiovascular fitness was in their "excellent" category, on a par with runners, swimmers and cyclists.

Bob Gajda, the 1966 Mr. America, popularized circuit training, a type of weight training that's particularly effective for developing cardiovascular fitness. In circuit training you do a group of exercises in rapid succession. Gajda would do one set of an exercise for one bodypart, then go immediately to another exercise for a different bodypart. For example, he might do 10 different exercises in succession, resting only long enough between them to get in position for the next one. Circuit training makes you puff and pant over an extended period of time, like running, but it also builds muscle.

Don't get the idea, however, that you can be a Mr. Olympia contender and also challenge Bill Rodgers in the Boston Marathon. The type of training that develops maximum muscle size won't develop maximum endurance, and vice versa. If you want cardiovascular fitness from your weight training, you should make it a point to train faster than usual and keep your heart rate up throughout your workouts. Then you'll develop a good balance of muscle and fitness.

Weight Training and Running

Q. I jog three days a week. I'm trying to have a basic workout with weight training also. How can I combine running and weight training for best results?

A. Bill Bowerman, University of Oregon track coach for 24 years and author of the book, *Jogging,* that started the running boom in this country, says in an interview in *The Runner* magazine that the biggest danger for either the beginning jogger or the world-class athlete is overtraining.

Bodybuilders often have the same problem. Weight training is the best way to build strength and muscle, and running or other aerobic activities like biking and swimming are the best ways to develop cardiovascular fitness. The combination of weight training with an aerobic activity like running is ideal—if you don't overdo it.

It's important to realize that rest is essential for progress both in weight training and running. The body responds to the stress of exercise by getting stronger, but the amount of exercise and the time allowed for rest determine the results.

I suggest that you first decide whether weight training or running is to be your primary activity. Since you've written to me, a bodybuilder, I'll assume your priority is weight training. Your objective, therefore, should be to obtain the cardiovascular benefits of running without interfering with your weight training. The key is moderation: Don't run so much that you can't recover in time for your next session with the weights.

I don't run because I don't like the pounding on my back and knees, but I do ride a bike. The way I combine bodybuilding and biking has application to your question. First, I always do my weight training before I ride because it's more important that I be fresh for my bodybuilding workout. If I'm going to ride hard, I've found it's best to do it the same day I train my legs and then take it easy the next day. This works better than lifting hard one day and then trying to ride hard the next. My rest day is for recuperation from weight training, not for wearing myself out with some other activity.

I continually monitor how I feel. If I'm tired when I work out with the weights or bike, I know I'm doing too much. From time to time I have ridden my bike so much that it interferes with my weight training. I've resigned myself to the fact that I can't weight train hard and bike hard at the same time. Through trial and error I've found that a moderate bike ride of about 30-45 minutes (increasing my heart rate to about 75 percent of maximum) five or six days a week maintains my aerobic fitness without interfering with my weight training. Experiment and find out what works best for you. Weight training and running are an ideal combination, but too much of a good thing will get you in trouble.

Stationary Biking for Bodybuilders

Q. You've mentioned that you ride a stationary bicycle, but you haven't given the details on how you do it. I just tighten my exercise bike down hard and pedal as long as I can. Am I doing it right?

The bike and I are practically fixtures in front of our TV. It's old hat to my son, Matt. *Photo by Wayne Gallasch.*

A. There's no fixed protocol for a bodybuilder to follow in riding a stationary bicycle, but I'll tell you some of the things I've learned since I bought mine in October of 1981. I started using an exercise bike to burn extra calories and keep my body fat down. I liked the stationary bike immediately, because it allowed me to easily burn 100 calories or more for each 10 minutes of riding time. If I wanted to push harder and burn calories faster and challenge my cardiovascular system more, it let me do that as well. Another thing that I liked about the bike was that it was easy on my joints. There's none of the jarring and pounding that I got from running. Nevertheless, I soon found that if I wasn't careful I could overdo it and interfere with my weight workouts. More about that in a minute; first I want to back up and tell you some other things about riding a stationary bicycle.

You'll enjoy it more if you ride in an interesting setting. I ride watching the TV. I understand that Frank Shorter concentrates so hard that he's content to pedal facing a blank wall, but I believe most people do better with some sort of outside stimulation. My wife's brother-in-law has a book rack on his bike. Others listen to classical music. It doesn't matter what you do, but do something you enjoy. I urge you to ride a quality bike for the same reason.

I always thought of a stationary bicycle as a toy until I tried a Tunturi Ergometer in the store where I eventually bought mine. It didn't look like much, but as soon as I experienced its quietness, control and precision I was hooked. Just as it's more fun to train on good weight training equipment, it's more pleasing to ride a fine exercise bike. If you can get by without a space age control panel, you can find an excellent bike in the $400-$600 price range. All you really need are gauges to tell you pedaling speed (RPM) and resistance (usually in watts); this will allow you to compare different workouts and measure progress.

A pulse meter mounted on the handlebars is also quite helpful. You can buy a good one for about $100 at a sporting goods store or a big department store. You need to know your heart rate, because it indicates how hard you're working and how many calories you're burning. For fat burning purposes, it's best to keep your pulse rate between 65 and 80 percent of maximum most of the time. Subtract your age from 220 to estimate your maximum heart rate. If you drop below this range you won't burn enough calories, and if you go higher you'll wear yourself out before you burn very many calories.

You control pulse rate by adjusting pedaling speed and resistance until you're in the proper range.

For me, one of the most appealing aspects of riding a stationary bike is control. You're not subject to shifts in the wind and traffic. You make your own hills and flats. With a little experience, you can completely control your body's response to the exercise.

To warm up, I pedal at a low resistance (75 watts) for two or three minutes. I also cool down for 5 or 10 minutes with almost no resistance, until my heart rate drops below 100. Not counting warm-up and cool-down, my rides last from 20 minutes to an hour. During the main part of the ride I change the pedaling resistance and check my heart rate, every five minutes. On hard days, I increase the pedaling resistance by 25 watts every five minutes, starting at 100 watts and working as high as 250. This takes my heart rate from a little over 100 to the 160-170 range. In my last hard bike session, after hitting 250 watts, I backed off to 200 watts, and then spent another 15 minutes working up to 250 again. Then I backed off to 200 for another five minutes, cooled down for about 10 minutes and called it a day.

I work this hard only once a week to increase my cardiovascular fitness. I do my hard rides on the same day I train my legs hard with the weights. This gives my body a hard jolt all at one time, and then allows plenty of time for recovery. On another day of the week, a medium leg training day, I do a medium workout on the bike lasting about 45 minutes and get my heart rate up to about 80 percent (200 watts). On the other days of the week, I take an easy workout lasting 20 or 30 minutes and go no higher than 150 or 175 watts (heart rate about 65 percent).

There's nothing magic about my bike routine, but it does illustrate several important points. First, be sure to spend a few minutes warming up and cooling down. Two or three minutes of warm-up allows your body to move gradually into the high heart rate of the actual workout. After you've finished, spending five minutes or more cooling down lets your heart rate decline gradually. Dr. Kenneth Cooper, author of the famous series of books on aerobic exercise, says, "The majority of severe cardiac irregularities that can be dangerous, occur following the exercise, not during it." According to Dr. Cooper, moving around for a few minutes after you finish exercising pumps the blood from the working muscles back into the central circulatory system.

112

Variety, during and between rides, is another important component of my routine. Time passes faster if you keep changing the pedaling resistance during the course of each ride. It's boring to pedal at the same resistance all the time.

You should also vary the intensity of your rides—you won't improve if you ride easy all the time, and you'll wear yourself out and probably get injured if you ride hard constantly. Every hard session should be followed by one or more easy sessions. This gives your body a chance to recover, and it's especially important for bodybuilders, who must have plenty of energy for their regular training sessions.

I've mentioned in this column before that it's probably impossible to be both a great endurance athlete and a great bodybuilder. Mr. Olympia would be no challenge to Rob de Castella or Alberto Salazar in the marathon and, of course, the reverse is also true. Choose one activity as your major activity, and then relegate the other to a secondary status. Don't let the tail wag the dog. Don't wear yourself out on the bike. Remember, for a bodybuilder weight training comes first.

For this reason, when I'm peaking as a bodybuilder I reduce the intensity of my biking sessions. I still use my bike to burn off body fat, but I save my major efforts for the weights. When bicyclists or other endurance athletes peak in their own sport, they back off on their weight training assistance exercises. By the same token, when a bodybuilder goes for a peak, he or she should let up on endurance assistance exercises.

A final word of caution: If you're out of shape, start slowly and gradually build up the length and intensity of your rides.

I hope I've helped you get more benefit and enjoyment out of your exercise bike. Good luck.

Heavyhands*: Four Limbs Are Better Than Two

Q. What's your opinion of the Heavyhands system of aerobic exercise developed by Dr. Leonard Schwartz, a Pittsburgh psychiatrist, and described in his book *Heavyhands, The Ultimate Exercise* (Little, Brown and Company: 1982)? Dr. Schwartz recommends the use of light dumbbells, 1-10 pounds, for high repetitions, up to 30 minutes or more, to develop overall fitness and

Heavyhands is a useful adjunct to my bodybuilding program. *Photo by Wayne Gallasch.*

burn calories. Would it be good for a bodybuilder?

A. I first learned of Heavyhands in Mike Lambert's *Powerlifting-USA* magazine. Intrigued by a system of aerobic exercise that uses the upper body as well as the legs, I read Dr. Schwartz's book and purchased some Heavyhands weights. I doubt that there is any one ultimate exercise, but I'm favorably impressed by Dr. Schwartz and his method.

Dr. Schwartz is no armchair exercise theorist. Starting at age 50, by the time he was 57, he had lowered his resting pulse rate from 80 to a phenomenal 38 and reduced his body fat from 15 percent to 4 percent. His oxygen uptake capacity moved up from what you would expect for a sedentary psychiatrist to a level on par with world-class marathon runners and cross-country skiers. His muscles aren't big, but his definition and muscularity would make any bodybuilder sit up and take notice. He looks extremely good for his age; actually, he looks good for a man half his age. Dr. Schwartz says Heavyhands has worked some physiological miracles on him, and I believe it.

Dr. Schwartz claims, and it seems logical, that working the arms and legs in combination consumes more oxygen and burns more calories than exercises that stress mainly the legs. Heavyhands is a way to work the whole body; with traditional aerobic exercises the upper body merely goes along for the ride. Working the arms and legs simultaneously activates a greater volume of muscle than working the legs alone. What it boils down to is that four limbs are better than two for expending calories and burning fat. An added bonus is that by working arms and legs in combination you can continue exercising a longer period at the same intensity than you can if you use only the legs. I'm interested in any system that allows me to burn more calories, and from that standpoint I'm convinced that Heavyhands has something to offer bodybuilders.

I switched from running to biking because it's easier on my body. As I've mentioned in this column before, I no longer run because I don't like the pounding on my back and knees. Heavyhands is another way to lessen wear and tear of aerobic exercise on the body. Spreading the stress over four limbs allows the body to take more exercise before experiencing the symptoms of overuse.

Most bodybuilders aren't interested in specializing in any particular type of aerobic exercise; they simply want to burn more calories without damaging their joints or tiring their muscles so much that they can't train properly. This is an advantage offered by Heavyhands, because the system allows different movements (Dr. Schwartz shows 100 or more in his book).

Still, I find that most Heavyhands exercises concentrate fatigue in the shoulders. For that reason I've adopted an eclectic approach to aerobics that allows me to exercise every day without causing stress or fatigue in any particular part of my body. For example, I ride my stationary bicycle one day, use my rowing machine the next, rebound on the third day and do Heavyhands on the fourth. This rotation system works well, and for a bodybuilder I believe it's better than sticking to any one type of aerobic exercise. It also keeps me from getting bored.

*HEAVYHANDS is a trademark of Leonard Schwartz, M.D.

Spread The Stress Of Fat-Burning Exercise

Q. Although I've been training for more than 20 years, I've learned a lot by reading your "Ripped" in *Muscle & Fitness.* I've also read your second book, *Ripped 2,* and I can truthfully say that it is the best training book I've ever read.

Recently I have incorporated another device into my training that you may find beneficial. On the days I don't run or weight train, I use a Schwinn Air-Dyne Ergometer. This is much better than a regular stationary bike in several ways:
- It has a push-pull arm motion that's synchronized with the pedals; thus
- You get more of a whole-body workout;
- The aerobic effect is far superior to the stationary bike or regular bike.

I would enjoy seeing your comments on the advantages of spreading the stress of aerobic exercise over the whole body.

A. Thank you for your kind comments. In the October, 1983, "Ripped," I wrote about Heavyhands, the system of aerobic exercise developed by Dr. Leonard Schwartz which uses light dumbbells to work the upper and lower body aerobically. Working the arms and legs together activates a greater volume of muscle than working the legs alone, and by spreading the stress over four limbs

The rower is another part of my arsenal of fat-burning equipment. *Photo by Wayne Gallasch.*

rather than two the body can take more exercise before experiencing overuse symptoms. A stationary bicycle that works both the upper body and lower body should have the same advantage.

In the September, 1983, issue of *The Runner* magazine, exercise physiologist David L. Costill, Ph.D., wrote how training can be made more effective: "What we need in developing the full capacity of the [body] is to find a way to stress the [body]... without traumatizing it.... We ought to be able to find ways to reduce the trauma so you can do more volume and tolerate more stress." That's the advantage of combining several different types of exercise to develop fitness and burn body fat. Running doesn't stress the upper body enough, and the pounding of the feet on the ground traumatizes the body. By combining upper and lower body biking with running you can fill Dr. Costill's prescription for more effective training, you can exercise more and harder without breaking down.

Dr. Stan James, an orthopedic surgeon who has operated on world class athletes like Mary Decker, Frank Shorter and four-time Olympic Hurdler Willie Davenport, also believes that the best way to become fit without injuring yourself is to spread the stress over different areas of the body. "My feeling," he said in the November, 1983, issue of *The Runner*, "is that running isn't the only answer to fitness. I would really like to see the American fitness scene become broader to include a variety of things.... I'm concerned that 10 or 15 years from now we might find more permanent problems occurring as a result of overuse."

Dr. James doesn't speak only from the clinical experience of treating runners and other athletes. A stress fracture of the pelvis forced him to broaden his own fitness program beyond running. He now bikes, roller skates and skis cross-country. He especially likes cross-country skiing because, as with Heavyhands and your Schwinn Air-Dyne, the upper body is exercised as well as the lower body. James says, "Cross-country skiers as a group have the highest oxygen uptake among athletes because of the total body effort." The variety of Dr. James' exercise program allows him to push his body well beyond the capacity of his legs to withstand the pounding of running.

That too much running will cause a loss of muscle size has long been a part of bodybuilding lore. Research reported in the November, 1983, issue of *The Physician and Sportsmedicine* magazine tends to support this view. Drs. Rudolph H. Dressendorfer and Charles E. Wade studied 12 male runners during a road race held over 20 days. Mileage averaged 17.3 miles per day, twice their regular training distance. For bodybuilders, the key finding of the study was that the unaccustomed mileage produced thigh muscle atrophy. According to the researchers, these runners sustained thigh muscle injury caused by chronic overuse. "We propose," they wrote, "that the . . . reduction in thigh girth resulted from decreased muscle fiber diameter. . . . In addition to the proposed breakdown of muscle protein, depletion of intramuscular substrates such as glycogen and triglycerides also could have contributed to the observed reduction in thigh girth." Significantly, the runners did not lose weight or body fat. The fat under the skin over the thighs remained the same. This suggests that a bodybuilder who engages in excessive running to lose body fat could very well end up losing muscle instead.

To sum up, I'm convinced that your addition of upper-body aerobic exercise to your weight training and running is a wise move. You'll be able to tolerate a greater volume of aerobic exercise and, therefore, burn more body fat by exercising both your arms and legs. Nevertheless, you should be sure to add upper-body exercise on your stationary bicycle gradually. Give your body a chance to adapt to the new stress. This will insure that you burn body fat, and that you don't copy the runners in the study described by destroying muscle tissue. You should also keep your heart rate below 80 percent of maximum most of the time so you'll burn mainly fat; a faster heart rate indicates that you're burning mostly muscle sugar, glycogen.

By the way, as a result of your letter I added the Schwinn Air-Dyne to my arsenal of aerobic exercise equipment. My program for staying lean and fit includes walking, biking, rowing, rebounding, Heavyhands, and now upper and lower body exercise on the Schwinn Air-Dyne.

Good luck on your training, and thanks for the excellent suggestion.

CHAPTER SEVEN

DEVELOPING A WELL-DEFINED WAISTLINE

CHAPTER SEVEN: DEVELOPING A WELL-DEFINED WAISTLINE

Chiseled Abdominal Area

Q. I have a problem with excess skin in the abdominal area. My abs are muscular, but I still don't have that tight, hard look. How can I get rid of the excess skin on my abs?

A. I am asked this question in various forms all the time. Everybody wants chiseled abs.

A common prescription is to train abs every day or even twice a day. But this is an absurd recommendation. No matter how many abdominal exercises you do, it won't melt the fat off your waistline; only diet and increased energy expenditure will do that. I train abs hard and heavy twice a week to develop muscular density and deep cuts. I don't increase sets or reps before a contest; I increase intensity. I do Bent-Knee Sit-Ups (on the steepest incline bench I can find, holding a dumbbell on my chest), Leg-Ups on the Leg Curl Machine, and heavy Dumbbell Side Bends. On all three exercises I do no more than two sets and use the heaviest weight I can for about 10 slow, controlled reps.

To remove any excess fat from my waistline and bring my abs out sharp and clear, I use a balanced, low-calorie diet and aerobic exercise.

Train the abs hard and heavy 2-3 times a week, cut back on your caloric intake and increase your overall activity level. Then you'll get the tight, hard abs you want.

The Negative Sit-Up

Q. I've been doing Sit-Ups and Leg Raises religiously, 100 or more reps every workout, but I still have no definition in my abdominal area. What do you suggest?

123

Abs like this are the result of heavy exercise plus diet and aerobics. *Photo by Bill Reynolds.*

I use the steepest abdominal board I can find and hold a dumbbell on my chest for added resistance. *Photo by Mike Neveux.*

A. Abs should be trained like any other bodypart—hard, briefly and infrequently. It's a common misconception that the waistline can be reduced by doing hundreds of Sit-Ups and Leg Raises. This doesn't work because fat is systemic; it's all over the body. In order to reduce fat on the waistline you must become lean all over. In short, fat is removed from the waist by dieting and increased calorie expenditure, not more abdominal exercise. Your objective should be to develop the abdominal muscles. Don't try to work them so much the fat will melt away. It won't.

My favorite abdominal exercise is the Negative Sit-Up. I do Bent-Knee Sit-Ups on the steep incline, holding a dumbbell on my chest. I do slow, controlled repetitions and I contract my abdominals hard at the top. I pay particular attention to lowering to the start of the exercise, the negative part: I lower my body slowly, so I can feel the action in my abdominals all the way down. I use a dumbbell that allows me to do 6-8 repetitions in regular style. When I reach positive failure, I switch to negative-only repetitions to further exhaust the abdominal muscles. Using my arms, I return the dumbbell, and then my body, to the top position. I continue with negative-only repetitions until I can no longer control the downward movement, about four additional repetitions. I rarely do more than two sets. Try the Negative Sit-Up and don't train your abs any more than you train your biceps or any other bodypart.

More On Training The Waist

Q. I've read your previous columns on training the abs, but I'd still like more details.

A. Apparently you're not alone, because I continue to receive many letters asking about training the waist. A well-muscled, sharply defined midsection is the hallmark of a quality physique; it's also the very essence of being ripped.

As I've said in this column before, many people believe the best way to train the abs is to do hundreds of Sit-Ups, Leg Raises and Twists, every day. That's wrong. Fat is removed from the waist by dieting and aerobic exercise, not by training the abs directly. If you have a layer of fat on your body, your abs will be covered by fat, no matter how many abdominal exercises you do. To bring out your abdominal muscles, you must do two things: (1) develop the muscles

On Side Bends I use a heavy dumbbell and bend over until the weight touches my foot. *Photo by Mike Neveux.*

I do Twisting Sit-Ups entirely to the side. I curl up on one side, lower on that side, and then curl and lower on the other side. *Photos by Wayne Gallasch.*

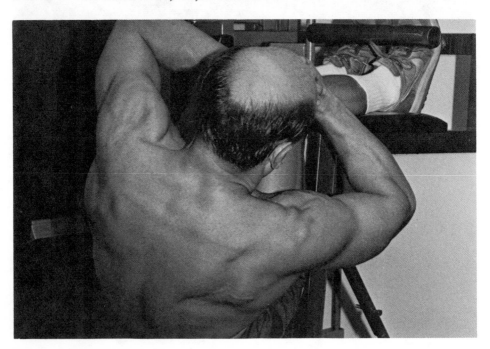

in the abdominal area through intense training, and (2) burn the fat off your whole body with diet and aerobic exercise so the abdominal muscles will show.

Train your abdominal muscles two or three times a week, just like any other body part. High repetitions are a waste of time. Best results come from two or three sets of each exercise using heavy resistance. If you can do more than 8-12 repetitions, you aren't using enough weight.

To develop the whole abdominal region, aim your training at three areas: upper abs, lower abs and the sides or obliques. I'll give you tips on training each area.

Done properly, the Incline Sit-Up is still the best exercise I know for the upper abs. Keep your knees bent and curl your body up into a ball. This is important. If you keep your knees and back straight and don't curl up, you work your hip flexor muscles, not your abs.

The front abdominal muscle, the rectus abdominis, originates in the pubic area and attaches at the ribs: when contracted it pulls the hips and the rib cage together. When you do Sit-Ups, concentrate on this short range of motion. Curl your body up slowly and under control. Contract the upper abs hard at the top and lower slowly. You should be able to feel the tension in your abs throughout the motion. Focus on shortening and lengthening the distance between the rib cage and hips.

It's a good idea to vary the angle of your Sit-Up Board, from very steep to almost flat on the ground. This changes the angle of stress on the abs. A steep incline puts maximum resistance on the abs at the top, fully contracted position. Therefore, to stress the abs earlier in the range of motion do Sit-Ups with your board at lower angles as well. You'll probably need to hold a dumbbell on your chest for added resistance, especially with the Sit-Up Board low.

For the sides, I like heavy Dumbbell Side Bends. I bend over until the dumbbell touches the side of my foot. I use a slow, controlled style, going down and up. I lower the dumbbell at about half the speed I use on the way up. For variety, I lower the dumbbell to the front to work the rear obliques, or to the rear to work the front obliques. When I do these variations I lower the dumbbell only to knee level. I suggest that you do all three variations of the Side Bend to work your obliques fully.

Don't worry about overdeveloping your obliques. I've used as much as 145 pounds in the Dumbbell Side Bend, and I haven't

Here's the start and finish of the Hip Curl. Note how I round my back and pull the hips up toward the rib cage. *Photos by Mike Neveux.*

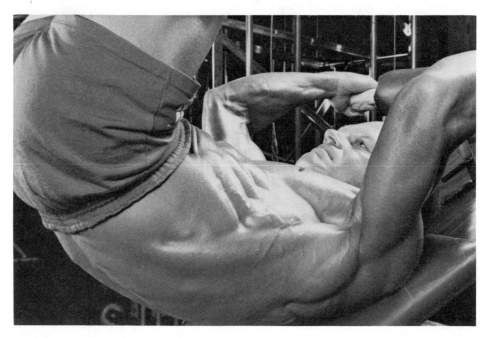

developed huge, unsightly obliques. It's probably impossible to develop obliques muscles that are too large. A layer of fat over the obliques is usually the problem, not overly large muscles. As I've already said, the remedy for that is diet and aerobic exercise.

Another good exercise for the sides is the Twisting Pulldown from a high pulley. This exercise is done from a kneeling position. The motion is like bowing with a twist. Using a rope handle, alternate from side to side bringing the elbows across the body and down by the opposite knee. Contract the muscles on the side of the waist hard at the bottom, and keep them under tension both on the downward and upward motion. You can hold the rope on either side of your head. This changes the angle of pull and stresses the side muscles differently.

The Twisting Sit-Up is another excellent exercise for the sides. To do my variation of this exercise you'll need a sturdy Sit-Up Board that won't tip to the side. I use a steeply inclined Sit-Up Board and anchor my feet firmly; twisting my body, I Sit-Up to the side, contracting my oblique muscles hard. I also lower my body to the side. The whole motion is done to the side. I curl up on one side, lower myself on that side, and then curl and lower on the other side. As before, I raise and lower myself slowly and under control to keep tension on the muscles throughout the motion. You'll like the feel of this exercise. Try it.

The Hip Curl on an abdominal board is my favorite exercise for the lower abs. Look at the photos to see how this exercise is performed. To keep tension on your lower abs, concentrate on pulling the hips up toward the rib cage. If you feel the tension go off the lower abs, you have either lowered or raised the hips too much. Again, do the exercise slowly and under control, on both the upward and downward motion. To increase the resistance use ankle weights.

For variety, the Hip Curl can be done while hanging from a chin bar or supporting yourself on a dipping stand. Again, concentrate on curling the hips up toward the rib cage.

I don't do conventional leg raises. To work the lower abdominals effectively the hips must be curled up toward the rib cage. Leg raises don't do this. They tighten, but don't shorten, the abdominal muscles. The leg raise works the hip flexor muscles; the abs act only isometrically as stabilizers. The Hip Curl is much better; it contracts the lower abs through their full range of motion.

Remember, don't try to sharpen your abs by training every day with endless reps and sets. Develop your abs with hard, brief training. And to burn the fat off so people can see your abs, use diet and aerobic exercise. With this type of routine, super abs are guaranteed.

CHAPTER EIGHT

PHYSIOLOGICAL FACTORS

CHAPTER EIGHT: PHYSIOLOGICAL FACTORS

The Ripped Metabolism

Q. My training partner says he has a slow metabolism and must keep his caloric intake extremely low to lose fat. He says that he's basically a fat person. Do some people have skinny metabolisms and others fat metabolisms?

A. Because of my extremely low body fat percentage, I've often heard it said that I must be blessed with a fast metabolism. I recently had my basal metabolic rate (BMR) measured to see if I really do have a "skinny metabolism." BMR is the rate at which the body burns energy while at rest. In other words, the BMR equals the number of calories the body requires to sustain its vital functions: heart beat, breathing, digestion, et cetera.

There's a rule-of-thumb formula to estimate BMR. For women: Add a zero to your weight and then add your weight. For men: Add a zero to your weight and then add twice your weight. At the time of the test I weighed 163. Using the formula, my expected BMR would be 1956 calories a day. (To 163 add a zero, giving you 1630, and to this figure add two times 163, or 326, for a total of 1956.) My BMR test showed that my total daily basal need is 2632 calories. In other words, it takes 2632 calories a day for my body to function at its most basic level. On "idle" I burn 676 more calories than would normally be expected.

Is my fast metabolism a happy accident? Did nature play a dirty trick on your training partner by giving him a slow metabolism? There's more to it than that. Diet and exercise can speed up your metabolism; a "fat metabolism" can be converted to a "skinny metabolism."

Most of the food you eat is burned by your muscles. This is true even when you're not exercising. Muscle cells burn calories even when you sleep. When you are active during the day, your muscle tissue burns more calories; and when you exercise, your muscles burn calories at a still faster rate. How many calories does fat burn?

For most of us, fast or slow metabolism is the result of our lifestyle. *Photo by Bill Reynolds.*

Fat cells are fairly inactive. They don't have nearly as many blood vessels in them as do active muscle cells, and they burn very few calories.

What happens if a person with 25 percent body fat and another person with three percent body fat both eat an equal number of calories per pound of bodyweight? The person with 25 percent fat will get fatter, while the person with three percent fat, and more calorie-burning muscle tissue, will get leaner. The person with three percent fat, in effect, speeds along on an eight-cylinder racing engine burning fuel like mad and the fat person operates on a four-cylinder economy model.

Your training partner may have a slow metabolism, but he can speed it up by reducing his body fat and increasing his muscle mass.

Another point for your training partner to consider is that aerobic exercise (walking, running, cycling, swimming, and other activities that elevate the breathing and heart rate for a prolonged period) increases the capacity of the body to burn fat. The benefits of aerobic exercise work for you 24 hours a day. If you are aerobically fit, you burn more body fat even when you sleep.

In 1977, when my body fat was first measured at 2.4 percent, it was also determined that my aerobic fitness level was 50 percent above average. Putting it another way, this means that my ability to burn body fat is 50 percent above average. Your training partner can speed up his fat-burning capacity by including aerobic exercise in his program.

A final caution to your training partner: Extremely low-calorie diets cause muscle loss. To function properly the brain must have glucose (blood sugar). Carbohydrates are the primary source of glucose. If your carbohydrate intake is too low, then protein can also be converted to glucose to supply your brain. Fat, however, cannot be converted to glucose. Fat is converted to fatty acids. Fatty acids feed your muscles, but they cannot replace the glucose which your brain must have. What happens if your diet doesn't contain enough carbohydrate or protein to supply your brain with glucose? If you reduce your caloric intake that much, body protein (muscle) is broken down and converted to glucose to feed your brain. This is no minor consideration, because when you're not exercising, your brain uses two-thirds of the glucose in your blood. Your training partner should lose weight slowly so the loss will be fat, not calorie-burning muscle tissue.

I've heard about people with naturally fast or slow metabolisms, and they probably do exist, but for most of us a fast or slow metabolism is the result of our lifestyle. Get ripped through sensible diet and exercise, like I did, and you'll find it easier to stay ripped. You'll have a "ripped metabolism."

Aerobics Can Lower Your Body Fat Setpoint

Q. I believe my metabolism is very slow because, as I discovered during a recent layoff, my weight and abdominal girth skyrocket if I just glance at food, so to speak. I've reduced my bodyweight by 55 pounds and my waist by 13 inches. By bodybuilding standards, however, I'm still carrying about 10 pounds of excess fat, and I'd like to lose as much of this as possible. What volume and frequency of aerobic exercise would be best to achieve my goal?

A. You're smart to focus on aerobic exercise to help you become really lean or, in bodybuilding terminology, "ripped." As you approach maximum leanness, the body becomes more resistant to fat reduction through diet. The body's survival mechanism comes into play, and the body starts handling food more efficiently to protect its fat stores. This is explained in *The Dieter's Dilemma— Eating Less and Weighing More* (Basic Books, Inc., 1982) by William Bennett, M.D., and Joel Gurin. Bennett and Gurin believe the body strives to maintain a body fat "setpoint."

The setpoint theory says that each of us has a genetically determined, but variable, internal mechanism that dictates how much fat we carry. This internal thermostat operates to maintain a "set" amount of fat on the body. When we attempt to reduce our body fat below our natural setpoint, this mechanism slows our metabolism and reduces our activity level so we can burn our food more efficiently and maintain our body fat level. On the other hand, when we accumulate fat above our setpoint, the body tends to speed up our basal metabolic rate and "waste" the calories we consume to bring our body fat back to the setpoint. This same mechanism increases our appetite when we fall below the setpoint and decreases it when we go above it.

One of the first major studies to indicate the existence of a body fat setpoint was conducted in 1944-45 by Ancel Keys at the University of Minnesota. The purpose of the study was to secure

140

information that would help in the rehabilitation of starved populations in the war zone. Keys kept 36 volunteers on a starvation diet (half their usual ration) for 24 weeks, until they lost about 25 percent of their starting weight and about half their body fat.

As you might expect, Keys' subjects became preoccupied with food. They were hungry all the time. Their lives revolved around mealtimes. They became apathetic and lethargic. They did everything they could do to avoid activity. In sum, they were miserable.

However, the most fascinating development came when refeeding began. Their food intake was gradually increased and they were allowed to gain weight. "Even so," Bennett and Gurin write, "they remained miserable.... Even though the men were now consuming more calories than they were burning each day, they were far from content." As a matter of fact, they stayed hungry and uncomfortable for more than six months, until they had returned to their starting weights and percentages of body fat.

The authors conclude that: "Keys' experiment provides some of the clearest evidence that the human body itself demands a certain amount of adipose tissue.... The psychological distress that accompanies starvation appears to come principally from reducing the body's store of fat to an amount below its setpoint, and the distress is relieved only when the full amount is replenished."

That's the bad news. The good news is that your body fat setpoint can be lowered. The first way to lower your setpoint is to avoid sweet and fatty foods. When our ancient ancestors came upon high-calorie foods, their setpoints went up. On the rare occasions when a rich source of calories presented itself, they were genetically programmed to overeat. This allowed them to deposit extra adipose tissue on their bodies to prepare for the next famine or epidemic. This is a survival mechanism we don't need, and by avoiding high-calorie foods we can keep our setpoint turned down.

Aerobic exercise is the other way to lower your setpoint. Aerobic exercise burns extra calories, but it does more than burn calories while you exercise: it speeds up your metabolism so you burn more calories long after you finish exercising. Aerobic exercise can increase your metabolism up to 25 percent for as long as 15 hours! It also has an appetite-regulating effect. Numerous studies on laboratory animals and humans have proven the effectiveness of aerobic exercise in weight control.

Bennett and Gurin cite a study of laboratory rats performed at Harvard School of Public Health. When made to run on a treadmill a few minutes a day, laboratory rats lost weight and ate slightly less than usual. An hour a day of gentle exercise on a treadmill reduced both their weight and food intake. When the rats were forced to run longer—between one and six hours a day—they ate more, but only enough to hold their new, low weight.

Humans react the same way to aerobic exercise. To lower your body fat setpoint, you must engage in aerobic exercise for at least 20 minutes at a time and you must also repeat the exercise fairly frequently. According to the authors of *The Dieter's Dilemma,* people who exercise four or five times a week lose three times faster than those who exercise only three days a week, and one or two weekly sessions are completely ineffective. They recommend daily aerobic exercise.

Personally, I walk for 45 minutes to an hour before breakfast six or seven days a week. I also ride my stationary bicycle for about 30 minutes before dinner five or six days a week. This program, combined with weight training and a sensible diet, allows me to maintain my body fat below six percent.

To lose that stubborn 10 pounds, I suggest 30 minutes to an hour of aerobic exercise at least five days a week—daily would be even better. A good goal to shoot for would be an hour of rapid walking, or 45 minutes of biking, or 30 minutes of jogging or comparable amounts of other aerobics every day.

Hormones in Men & Women

Q. I understand that the male sex hormone allows men to develop bigger muscles than women. I'd like to know more about this.

A. Hormones do account for the difference in potential for muscular development between men and women. A woman bodybuilder can't develop muscles like Arnold, but most men can't either. Some women have higher hormone levels than other women and the same is true for men. The average man, however, has about 35 percent more muscle-building hormones (androgenic hormones) than the average woman.

In both men and women the adrenal cortex produces androgenic

142

hormones. The male advantage is because his testes also produce testosterone, the male sex hormone and the most potent androgenic hormone.

Carl Miller, former coach of the U.S. Olympic style weightlifting team, traveled extensively in Russia and Bulgaria, the top Olympic lifting countries. Carl tells me Russian and Bulgarian coaches use a number of tests to determine weight-lifting potential. One thing they check in their athletes is androgenic hormone level, one measure of bodybuilding potential. Bodybuilders can do the same thing.

Androgenic hormones are broken down in the body and appear in the urine as 17-ketosteroids. Normal adult men produce 7-20 milligrams of 17-ketosteroids each day. For adult women, the normal range is 5-15 milligrams per day. The higher you are in the range, the greater your potential.

If you are interested, your doctor can have your 17-ketosteroid production measured. The amount of testosterone in the blood can also be measured. Don't be discouraged, however, if you don't have a high androgenic hormone level. Determination and many other factors play a large part in bodybuilding success. You can improve dramatically through intelligent weight training and proper diet, no matter what your hormone level.

UPDATE:

According to Robert Kerr, M.D., an expert on the use of anabolic steroids with athletes, 17-ketosteroids in the urine is a poor test for androgen activity. Kerr says it's more a measure of adrenal gland function than testicular activity.

For the purpose of determining androgenic hormone level, Dr. Kerr prefers a sperm count or a blood test for serum testosterone. The drawback of the blood test is that it's expensive, at $60.00 or more.

Testosterone Level After Vasectomy

Q. In the December, 1980 issue of *Muscle & Fitness* you explained that men can develop bigger muscles than women because the testes produce testosterone, the most potent androgenic hormone. My wife and I don't want to have any more children and I am thinking about having a vasectomy. Will this operation affect my testosterone production, or decrease my ability to build muscle?

A. I can understand your concern. Testosterone is the most important muscle-building hormone and a key factor in bodybuilding.

A number of studies have been done to determine whether having a vasectomy affects male hormonal function or testosterone levels. Probably the most extensive investigation was carried out in Australia and reported in *Fertility and Sterility* (Vol. 31, No. 5, May 1979). The testosterone level of 54 healthy men was measured before they had a vasectomy and then for five years following the operation. Blood samples were taken immediately before vasectomy and at intervals of three, 12, 24, 36, 48 and 60 months thereafter. The investigators were unable to find any evidence that vasectomy reduces the amount of testosterone the testicles release into the bloodstream.

Other smaller studies also report no significant alteration in the subjects' testosterone levels after a vasectomy.

You should, of course, discuss all aspects of this matter with your doctor before you make a decision.

Two-Day Lag Rule

Q. I've noticed that I often feel good the day after I workout, but the next day, when it's time to workout again, I'm sore and tired. Is this unusual? What should I do about it?

A. It's not unusual at all. You're encountering the "two-day lag." When I was a teenager my father, a physician, called my attention to the lag between the workout and the time when the full effects are felt. To illustrate, he pointed out that when someone is knocked around in an automobile accident, he's sore and stiff the next day, but it's usually not until a day or two later that he has maximum discomfort. World-class runner Marty Liquori talks about the lag in his *Guide for the Elite Runner*. He says, "It usually takes at least one day and more often two for effects (injuries or fatigue) of a hard workout or race to hit you." I almost always feel the effects of a workout two days later. That's when my body really feels "used."

Being aware of the lag helps in planning and evaluating workouts. My legs may feel good after a heavy leg workout, but I know that doesn't mean that it's time to hit legs again. I know I should wait.

You should plan your workouts with the two-day lag in mind. If you're working your whole body on Monday, Wednesday and Friday, then Wednesday is probably the day you'll be dragging. Take it easy on your mid-week workouts and then go hard again on Friday. The four-day split system also takes the two-day lag into account. On this schedule you work half your body on Monday, rest that part of your body for two days, and then train it again on Thursday. The other half of the body is worked on Tuesday and Friday.

To succeed, a bodybuilder must learn to listen to his or her body. But, as the two-day lag indicates, body cues are sometimes difficult to interpret. They are tricky. However, if you listen carefully and regularly, you can usually figure out what your body is trying to tell you.

Muscle Soreness

Q. Is it true that muscle soreness means that my muscles are torn?

A. The technical term for the localized muscle soreness that appears 24-48 hours after unaccustomed exercise is "myositis." It was first hypothesized around the turn of the century that myositis is caused by microscopic tears in muscle or connective tissue. Until very recently there was no direct evidence for this theory.

Then, in 1977, Dr. W.M. Abraham reported finding substances in the urine that represented connective tissue damage when delayed muscle soreness was present. These substances were significantly higher during maximal soreness. This was the first strong evidence of the structural damage theory of muscle soreness.

More recently Dr. David Costill, head of the Human Performance Laboratory at Ball State University in Muncie, Indiana, reported on a study that his laboratory and exercise physiologists at Ohio University, Athens, Ohio, conducted with marathon runners. Using an electron microscope, the researchers examined muscle biopsies taken from the calves of 10 highly trained male runners before and after a marathon for structural damage. Writing in *The Runner* magazine, Dr. Costill gave these startling results: "In nearly all the samples studied, including those taken before the race, there was evidence of muscle fiber death (necrosis) and inflammation within the muscle."

These conditions were most pronounced at one and three days after the race when the most severe muscle soreness was present. Dr. Costill believes that eccentric contractions that occur during running are what caused the damage. In running, especially downhill, there are movements that involve lengthening of the muscle at the same time the muscle is attempting to shorten. Costill says, "The muscles are attempting to shorten but are literally pulled apart. Consequently, the connective tissues in the muscles and muscle membranes are physically torn apart."

Dr. Costill and his fellow researchers suggest that these muscle tissue tears may be a major factor in post-exercise soreness.

Significantly, Dr. Costill has also studied the muscles of highly trained cyclists under the electron microscope, but found no indication of muscle fiber damage. Thus, it appears that some muscle soreness, especially where sudden strain or jerking movements are involved, is caused by tears in the muscle and connective tissue. However, this probably occurs less often than exercise physiologists once believed.

Herbert A. deVries, in the third edition of *Physiology of Exercise,* a standard text used in upper-level college courses, says that most delayed soreness following exercise is caused by spasm. Electromyography (EMG) studies show that muscle soreness is usually accompanied by spasm and that both the spasm and the soreness are relieved when the muscle is stretched. In fact, researchers can bring about muscle soreness experimentally and relieve it by static stretching.

Dr. deVries says that fatigued and overloaded muscles tend to shorten (probably due to a delayed swelling in the connective tissue). This results in a decrease in the blood supply to the muscle, causing a localized tissue anemia known as ischemia. The resulting blood deficiency produces pain. A vicious cycle is created, because the pain brings about a further shortening of the muscle and decrease in blood supply, which produces more pain.

There is no question, says Dr. deVries, that this cycle of pain is broken by stretching. The fact that muscle soreness is relieved by static stretching strongly suggests that the soreness is caused by spasm.

I'm sure most bodybuilders have noted, as I have, that almost any new exercise produces soreness, even if you've been training the involved muscle regularly. It seems that the body has to adjust to the new angle of stress and that muscle soreness is a part of the adjustment process. Your muscles are simply telling you that they're experiencing a new stress. After you do the new exercise a time or two, your body adjusts and the soreness goes away. This is the type of soreness that most bodybuilders experience, and it's probably caused by muscle spasm and not structural damage.

You can minimize soreness by warming up carefully, by avoiding sudden and jerky movements and by getting used to new exercises gradually. When soreness comes, static stretching usually gives relief.

Vascularity

Q. I read your book and almost all of your articles, but I've never seen anything written by you concerning vascularity. How did you develop your excellent vascularity?

A. I haven't written about vascularity because I don't do anything special to develop it. I find that my regular program of training and dieting removes the fat from my body and makes my veins visible.

If your body fat is down to a very low percentage and you're still not vascular, the problem may be hereditary. Some people have bigger and more prominent veins than others. For example, Clint Beyerle, a former Mr. USA, is probably the most vascular bodybuilder I've ever seen. His veins, particularly in his shoulders and pecs, stand out like highways on a road map. On the other hand, some bodybuilders are lean and muscular but still don't have outstanding vascularity.

Like my father, I have very prominent veins in my forearms. My wife, on the other hand, has small veins. Our nine-year-old son was recently in the hospital to have his tonsils removed. He didn't seem to mind the surgery, but he sure complained about the nurse sticking him several times before she could find his vein. He apparently inherited my wife's small veins.

Bodybuilding can increase the size and number of the blood vessels, and this will improve your vascularity. Bodybuilding increases demand for blood in the muscles. This demand causes an increase in total blood volume and in the size and number of blood vessels. When trained, the muscles require more oxygen and other nutrients, and also produce more carbon dioxide and other waste products. The blood brings oxygen and nutrients to the muscles and carries away waste products. Continual training increases the efficiency of this blood transport system. Dr. Kenneth Cooper described this phenomenon in his famous book *Aerobics*: "It's as if our dairy had improved its regular routes of delivery, expanding them into superhighways, and opened up newer and smaller routes into the boondocks."

Don't worry about your vascularity. Become as lean and muscular as you can through sensible diet and training. The vascularity will take care of itself.

The Pump

Q. How important is "the pump" in developing muscle?

A. Arnold may be right that the pump is second only to orgasm as a pleasurable sensation, but it's not all it's cracked up to be in the muscle building process. It's not the key factor.

Frequently an acquaintance I haven't seen for some time asks me if I'm still "pumping iron." I smile and say, "Yes," but I'm usually a little annoyed by the implication that a bodybuilder's muscles are something akin to puffed wheat.

A pump results from any type of muscular work that increases circulation and causes a buildup of waste products in the muscles. You can pump your arm like mad with a 15-pound dumbbell, but you won't build big arms. Doing 10 curls with the heaviest weight you can handle will also pump your biceps, but it will also make your biceps grow. Maximum effort, not maximum pump, builds muscle.

Any of you who have seen photos of David Rigert, the Russian weight lifting champion, or almost any other world class Olympic lifter, must have noticed their awesome musculature, particularly in the traps, lower back and thighs. Olympic lifters make no effort to achieve a maximum pump. They use heavy weights and low reps. They concentrate on lifting heavier and heavier weights. Rarely do they get a pump and, nevertheless, they build huge, impressive muscles.

Pumping Iron, the book and the motion picture, brought much well deserved attention to the sport of bodybuilding, but that title only scratches the surface of what it takes to build a championship physique. "The Pump" is nice, but it's not the whole story—not by a long shot!

Lift Fast For Fast-Twitch Fibers?

Q. I've heard that I should lift fast to develop my fast-twitch muscle fibers and slow to develop my slow-twitch fibers. Is this true?

A. Actually there are four types of muscle fibers: Type I, Type IIA, Type IIB and Type IIC. However, the three Type II fibers are usually lumped together and called fast-twitch muscle fibers. The Type II fibers differ in terms of resistance to fatigue, but none of them has the long-term endurance of the Type I fibers, the slow-twitch fibers.

We all have fast-twitch and slow-twitch muscle fibers, but some of us have a predominance of one type of fiber over the other. Champion distance runners usually have a high percentage of slow-twitch muscle fibers. Alberto Salazar, the world record holder in the marathon, has 92 percent slow-twitch fibers. His high percentage of enduring, slow-twitch fibers is a key factor in making him a champion in his sport. On the other hand, champion sprinters usually have a higher percentage of fast-twitch muscle fibers. The distribution of slow-twitch and fast-twitch fibers is genetically determined. It can't be changed. If you're born with a high percentage of slow-twitch fibers, you'll probably be a good long-distance runner, and if you have a high percentage of fast-twitch fibers, you'll be a good sprinter.

Fast-twitch muscle fibers contract 2-4 times faster than slow-twitch fibers. Nevertheless, both types of fibers are capable of contracting quite fast. The fast-twitch fibers are less resistant to fatigue than the slow-twitch fibers. The slow-twitch fibers have greater endurance, but the fast-twitch fibers contract with greater force.

Studies concerning the response of skeletal muscles to weight training are somewhat meager, but we do know—this is what you're interested in—that weight training primarily affects the fast-twitch fibers. Weight training makes the fast-twitch fibers hypertrophy (increase in size). Endurance exercise increases the aerobic capacity of the slow-twitch fibers, but has little effect on muscle size. To confirm this for yourself, check out a field of marathon runners: they don't have big muscles. On the other hand, sprinters tend to have good muscle size because they have trained their fast-twitch fibers. Weightlifters and bodybuilders are the extreme example of growth in fast-twitch muscle fibers as a result of high-intensity exercise.

From what I've said, it's clear that if big muscles are your goal, you should concentrate on developing your fast-twitch muscle fibers. Although it may seem logical that fast movements would develop fast-twitch fibers, that isn't necessarily the case. Both slow-twitch fibers and fast-twitch fibers are capable of moving extremely fast. Force of contraction, not speed of contraction, is the main difference between the two types of fibers. Slow-twitch fibers can move quite fast if the force requirements are low. If the force requirements are high, as in weight training, slow-twitch fibers can't do the job. It's when the force requirements are high, as when you're lifting a heavy weight, that the fast-twitch fibers are activated.

Muscle fibers work in a certain order. The smallest fibers, the slow-twitch fibers, are called on first, and the largest fibers, the fast-twitch fibers, are recruited last. It's the force, the load, that determines which muscle fibers will be used. If you lift a light weight fast, you'll activate your slow-twitch fibers and you'll see little muscle growth. You can curl a 15-pound dumbbell fast all day without developing any muscle size. But you'll develop an enduring biceps because you're using your slow-twitch fibers. To activate your fast-twitch fibers and make your biceps grow, you have to curl a heavy weight. You have to make high-intensity demands on your muscles to increase the size of your fast-twitch fibers. You can't do this with light, fast movements.

When you curl a weight fast, you're using momentum, not muscle. You're throwing the weight up. You're loading the muscle at the beginning of the movement and again at the end, but you're making no demands on the muscle during the rest of the movement. To make maximum demands on a muscle, you must load it throughout the range of movement. The only way to do this is with slow controlled movements.

To sum up, don't worry about your slow-twitch fibers; they won't grow to any noticeable degree. Don't try to do your exercises fast because you'll activate few fibers—slow-twitch or fast-twitch. Fast movements simply don't train your muscles effectively. It takes slow, high-intensity or high-force movements to activate your fast-twitch fibers and make your muscles grow. Fast, low-force movements are okay for marathoners, but not for bodybuilders. The bottom line for bodybuilders is: lift heavy and slow.

CHAPTER NINE

PSYCHOLOGICAL FACTORS

CHAPTER NINE: PSYCHOLOGICAL FACTORS

Inspiration

Q. Your body is fantastic—symmetrical, well-defined, developed, not over-developed. I hope someday my body will look as good as yours. Thanks for the inspiration!

A. I have received many letters like yours. I really appreciate the compliments. People like you inspire me to be a better bodybuilder. Letters like these make me think about the factors that have kept me training for more than 25 years. Do I train to improve fitness and health? Am I trying to increase my longevity? Or am I a competitive fanatic, training for a better-looking, stronger body? I know I train for all these reasons, but there is more.

Dr. George Sheehan, running's number one guru, says that people won't exercise just because it's good for them. Sheehan contends that inspiration is the key to motivating people to train for peak performance.

When I started training at age 13 I was motivated to become stronger than my school buddies. I think I felt a little inferior. I see the same thing in my eight-year-old son when he plays with the big kid across the street. The other day my son called me at the office and asked me to give him an exercise program so he could "get some muscle." I'd like to think that he wants to follow in my footsteps, but I know that my son really wants approval from his peers. The bigger and stronger kids inspire him to want "some muscle."

By the time I was a sophomore in high school I was stronger than any of my friends, so I set my sights higher. I vividly remember a high school assembly where an upper classman was honored for winning the State High School Pentathlon Championship, a five-event contest consisting of push-ups, chin-ups, jump reach, bar vault, and 300-yard shuttle run. His win inspired me. I made up my mind that I'd win that award the next year—and I did.

In later years lifting champions such as Steve Klisanin, Norbert

My early training years were devoted mainly to the three Olympic lifts: the Press, Snatch and Clean and Jerk. I still incorporate exercises like the Squat and Deadlift which work large muscle groups simultaneously. *Photo by Mike Neveux.*

Schemansky, Tommy Kono, Dave Sheppard, Isaac Berger and Chuck Vinci inspired me to excel in Olympic lifting.

Then, when I watched Vic Seipke win the 1976 Past-40 Mr. America title, I was inspired to enter a physique competition. I'd seen Vic win the 1955 Junior Mr. America contest, and he looked as good in 1976 as he did in 1955. I decided if Seipke could be at his best when he was over 40, I could, too. I went on to win my class at the Past-40 Mr. USA and the Past-40 Mr. America contests.

The desire to be healthy and fit has been a factor in my training. But it's inspiration that makes me want to improve each year. Without inspiration, I wouldn't be looking better than I ever have— at age 43. I wouldn't be Ripped.

Inspiration—it will make you a winner, too.

Motivation

Q. You've been training for a long time. What motivates you to keep going?

A. After 30 years, training has become an integral part of my life. I wouldn't be happy if I didn't train. However, my motivation comes from continually setting and achieving realistic goals based on previous performance.

An individual usually won't train to the point of habit unless he or she has already achieved some success along the way. In general, people set their goals a little higher than the level they are sure of attaining, and that's okay. Others, however, aim well beyond their capacities, setting their goals unrealistically high. These are the beginners who immediately aspire to become Mr. or Miss Olympia. Without goal gratification, they eventually drop out.

Almost every bodybuilder makes obvious gains at the start of training. Where the beginning bodybuilder aims next determines whether training motivation is likely to continue. Fortunately, my training efforts have been continually rewarded.

When I started to lift weights at 13 years of age, I wanted to be as strong as my athletic friends. After I achieved that goal, I aimed for, and won, the State High School Pentathlon Championship. The local newspaper ran a story headlined, "BASS IS STRONGEST." I was on my way. Success at the state, regional and national levels, in that order, followed. This early step-by-step success, I am

I plan for success by noting my goals for the next workout in my training diary. *Photo by Wayne Gallasch.*

Step-by-step success has kept me training for more than 30 years. Plus I enjoy exercise. *Photo by Bill Reynolds.*

convinced, is the basic reason for my training longevity.

To keep moving closer to your bodybuilding potential, take it one step at a time. Don't aim too high or too low. Raise your sights higher and higher, but slowly, and strive for good progress.

There is an additional, and equally important, requirement for training longevity—enjoyment. Physical effort must be a positive experience. If you don't enjoy using your body, you lessen your chance of training survival. In a recent article for *The Runner,* Frank Shorter wrote that from January, 1970, to December, 1980, he averaged 120 miles of running per week. That's more than 17 miles a day for more than a decade! Shorter gave a number of reasons why he put so much time and effort into training, but he concluded by saying he couldn't have done it if he didn't enjoy running.

Many who were star athletes in their teens and 20s discontinued the training habit in later life. The primary reason: They didn't really like physical effort. These early athletes participated in sports for peer approval, fame or money, but they never really appreciated the good feelings that exercise brings. The athletes who continue to train into their 30s and beyond, like Frank Shorter, simply enjoy exercise. I know I do. I wouldn't feel right if I didn't train.

One final suggestion: Try to make every training session a satisfying and rewarding experience. Structure your workouts so they will produce a feeling of accomplishment. The key is to set realistic workout-to-workout goals.

After every training session I write my goals for the next session in my training diary. It's not a complicated record. While the workout is fresh in my mind, I simply use an arrow to indicate whether I should repeat a movement with the same weight and reps, increase the weight or reps, or whatever. I don't hesitate to decrease the weight or reps if necessary. Remember, I'm setting myself up for a positive experience.

I make a point of graduating from one training success to another. It takes some planning, but it works. It has worked for me for 30 years. It will work for you, too.

Habits

Q. I can't seem to stay in the groove. I work out and diet for a while, but then I always seem to get diverted before I make any real headway. Do you have any suggestions that will help me stick with my training program?

A. You've got a lot of company. Somerset Maugham once said, "The unfortunate thing about this world is that good habits are so much easier to give up than bad ones."

In the 1950s, when I first started training, there was a health club that generated most of its income by selling lifetime memberships at ridiculously low prices. The owners knew that most members would train for a while and then quit. However, it doesn't have to be that way.

Most of us are creatures of habit. We tend to adopt a pattern of living which leads to the development of habits. The secret to success in body building is to make training and dieting a habit.

I recently spent several days with Bill Pearl at his new headquarters in Oregon. I was amazed when he told me that he had not missed more than 100 workouts since he won the Mr. America title in 1953. That's almost 30 years of regular training! Bill conducts his training like a business. It's his number one priority. He gets up

160

at 4:00 a.m. and trains before he does anything else. As he puts it, he takes care of himself first and then he takes care of his other obligations.

You may not want to get up at 4:00 a.m. to train but, with planning and discipline, you can make good nutritional habits and regular exercise part of your life.

Stress & Exercise

Q. In *Ripped 2* and in your cassette tape 3, you explain how training helps keep your life in focus and how everything else falls into place when you have training to fall back on. Well, I know what you mean by that, because I lost my 17-year-old boy in an accident seven months ago: If it wasn't for training with weights I would never have made it through. You should tell readers of your column in *Muscle & Fitness* how bodybuilding can help in the control of stress.

A. A major life-change event, such as the death of a spouse or close family member, divorce or even pleasant things, such as marriage, pregnancy or a new home, causes a great deal of stress. Furthermore, experts believe that chronic, everyday strains, such as facing a deadline or being caught in a traffic jam, can be equally stressful if not handled properly. An exercise program can help relieve the anxiety and tension that is caused by everyday stresses or brought about by a major tragedy such as you experienced.

In general, says Dr. Edward D. Greenwood, psychiatrist at the Menninger Clinic, exercise promotes a sense of well-being by enhancing ego strength, dissipating anger and hostility, relieving boredom and resolving frustration.

Time magazine recently carried an excellent cover story on stress. A recurring theme throughout the article was the factor of control: We live in a world of uncertainties and the feeling of lack of control of our lives is a major cause of stress. Exercise doesn't remove the uncertainties, but it certainly does help us cope with them.

The heart of most stress-management techniques is relaxation. Exercise, like transcendental meditation, self-hypnosis and biofeedback, elicits what Harvard cardiologist Herbert Benson, the guru of therapeutic relaxation, has termed the "relaxation response."

Dr. Hans Selye, the father of stress research, discovered that stress brings about the release of chemicals (epinephrine and norepinephrine) in the body, which are designed to prepare us for "fight or flight." Exercise helps to prevent the build-up of these "high-voltage" chemicals and aids in dissipating them once they are there. When our ancient ancestors would be confronted with a saber-toothed tiger, for example, these stress chemicals helped them to fight or run. Modern man, more often than not, has no outlet for his flight-or-fight mechanism, and that's where exercise comes in. Exercise is the modern equivalent of throwing a rock at the saber-toothed tiger and thereby allows for the release of tension that builds up, letting relaxation take place. In short, exercise provides an outlet for the stress response; it allows us to channel and control stress.

To give a concrete example, the 30 minutes I spend on my stationary bicycle most evenings before dinner makes me feel like a new man. No matter how tired or tense I am when I get home, I know that I'll feel better after I've been on my bike for a few minutes. Maybe it's the "high" runners talk about, but the world seems better after my stationary bike session. Similarly, the hour or so I spend in my gym most mornings calms me for the rest of my day. In my gym I'm in control, and that helps me cope with the uncertainties I face on the outside.

I can well understand how bodybuilding helped you cope with the loss of your son. It made you feel better about yourself, took your mind off the tragedy and made you relax. I'm glad that your bodybuilding helped you through this difficult period, and I hope your experience will help others cope with life's stresses, big and small.

Curing Burnout

Q. I seem to be losing my enthusiasm for bodybuilding. For a number of years I trained really hard and won several titles, but now I'm finding it very hard to stick with my diet and training. What can I do to get up for bodybuilding again?

A. It sounds like you're burned out, at least temporarily. Burnout in sports has been reported often in the news recently. Tennis superstar Bjorn Borg retired at only 26, and Dick Vermeil, who took his team to the Superbowl two years ago, retired as coach at 46. In bodybuilding, Mike Mentzer, in top form and still getting better, has announced that he's no longer interested in competing. Even Boyer Coe, one of the sport's most enduring stars, known for always being in shape and competing often, is now considering dropping out of competition.

I don't know the details behind the decisions made by these men, but it's interesting to contemplate why Bjorn Borg quits at 26, while Jimmy Conners is still competing at 30; or why Mike Mentzer stops competing at 30 while Chris Dickerson goes on to win the Mr. Olympia at 43. Or what makes Joe Weider at 62—now busier than ever publishing magazines and running Weider Health and Fitness—works out four times weekly. Or why Jack LaLanne is still going strong at 68.

The causes of burnout aren't fully understood, but psychologists and physicians who specialize in sports medicine agree that a primary cause is unrelenting pressure—stress over a long period of time.

Larry Armstrong, a doctoral fellow at Ball State University's Human Performance Laboratory, says, "It's probably a combination of mental and physical, but we know more about the mental aspects. How you treat it depends on how soon you want to bring them back. It's best to rest or find diversions."

According to Ronald L. Smith, a professor of clinical psychology at the University of Washington, coach Vermeil might have avoided burning out "if he had developed some other stress management skills—learned to get out from under the job a bit."

This explains why young swimmers who are required to practice twice a day from a very early age get sick of their sport and drop out by the time they reach college. They aren't allowed to take time off to have fun doing the things other kids do. Even the 25 million dollars he's made since 1974 wasn't enough incentive to keep Borg practicing tennis four hours a day. The endless tennis season became more than he was willing to tolerate. After 10 years as a pro, Borg said, "Tennis has to be fun if you are to get to the top, and I don't feel that way any more."

One reason Bill Pearl has remained at the top level of bodybuilding for so long is that he was careful not to compete too frequently. From his first competition in 1952 until his 1971 Professional Mr. Universe victory, he competed only 11 times. In the time that elapsed between his forays into competition, Pearl developed an interest in old cars and attended to the needs of members of his gym.

You probably need rest and relaxation. Forget about diet and training for a while. Have some fun. My guess is that it won't be long before your urge to train returns and you aim for your next contest.

To avoid burnout in the future, include rest and diversion in your program. It's important to take extended breaks from hard training on a regular basis. You should enjoy your training. When it becomes a grind, it's time to take it easy for a while.

Deprivation

Q. I've tried all kinds of diets, but I always get burned out and gain back any weight I've lost. Why can't I control myself? Is it my lack of willpower?

A. Geneen Roth in her fascinating book about compulsive eating, *Feeding the Hungry Heart* (The Bobbs-Merrill Company, 1982), says that diets don't work because they are based on deprivation. She maintains that "A binge is the other side of a diet; it is built into it; it is inevitable. For every diet there is an equal and opposite binge." She recommends that you forget about dieting and start listening to your body. She claims that with practice your body will tell you what and when to eat and, most importantly, when to stop.

Roth is on the right track. That's why I espouse the eating of natural foods that do not interfere with your body's ability to tell you when you've had enough. Processed foods with added sugar or fat and no fiber stimulate the appetite and encourage overeating.

To diet successfully you must avoid feeling deprived. So go easy on yourself. Go ahead and binge occasionally if that will relieve those built-up feelings of deprivation. It's also extremely important that you lose weight slowly. If you try to lose too fast you'll surely feel deprived and go off your diet.

If you reduce slowly and avoid appetite-stimulating foods you won't feel deprived and you'll probably be able to stay on your diet.

Fear Of Fat

Q. I am 15 years old and in the hospital right now suffering from anorexia nervosa. I've been here for close to three months and they're trying to put some weight on me. One of my problems is that I'm afraid of getting fat.

I want to put on some weight, but I want it to be good, solid muscle. Before when I wanted to get more definition I would just do about 600 Sit-Ups and 200 Push-Ups in the course of a day and not eat. This worked, but here at the hospital I'm not allowed to do this. Please, Mr. Bass, I need your help.

A. I'm not an expert on anorexia nervosa (an hysterical aversion to food, which may lead to serious malnutrition), but I do know that the fear of being fat is a serious problem in our society.

In her *Nutrition Book* (W.W. Norton & Company, 1981), Jane Brody, the personal health columnist of the *New York Times,* has this to say about anorexia nervosa: "It afflicts 10 times as many girls as boys, and is characterized by zealous dieting (sometimes interspersed with gorging), rapid weight loss beyond what everyone (except the dieter) would consider attractive, and the conviction that no matter how thin the dieter gets, she's [he's] still too fat.... If malnutrition becomes too severe, hospitalization may be necessary to correct the life-threatening effects of starvation and to start the patient eating again." Brody emphasizes that it's extremely important to seek professional help for this ailment.

Anorexia nervosa usually afflicts teenagers, but the fear of fat is much more widespread and affects people, especially women, of all ages. Fat is a major national issue, according to Margaret Mackenzie, a medical anthropologist at the University of California who has written a book on the subject soon to be published by Columbia University Press. A non-issue in many societies, fat is seen by Americans as bad; thin is good. Mackenzie says it's part of our moral code. Body fat is more than whether we're in control of our eating and our activity; for many of us, it's an index of control over all aspects of our lives. "When I'm in control of my eating, I'm in control of my life."

I expressed a similar thought in *Ripped 2,* when I said that my training gives me a general feeling of control. My bodybuilding is an important part of the positive view I have of myself. It's part of what allows me to say, "I'm okay." I know I'm not alone when I feel better

I keep my body fat very low, but I never starve myself. *Photo by Guy Appelman.*

about myself because I'm lean and muscular. As I've said before, I wouldn't feel right facing the world with atrophied muscles and a pot belly.

In our society, there's no denying the fact that thin is in. Like it or not, says Margaret Mackenzie, "If you're fat and you're upwardly mobile, you'll be discriminated against. You'll have trouble getting the best jobs, they'll look at you askance" wherever you go.

A real problem arises when we try to become lean, and feel bad about ourselves when we fail. You tried not eating and doing Sit-Ups and Push-Ups all day long, and ended up in the hospital. Many others diet on-and-off all their lives with meager results. They build up feelings of deprivation which cause them to go off their diets and gain back all the weight they lost, and more. For many, as Geneen Roth wrote in her book, *Feeding the Hungry Heart* (The Bobbs-Merrill Company, Inc. 1982), "For every diet there is an equal and opposite binge."

In spite of the many failures, efforts to lose body fat don't have to result in illness or despair. There are healthy ways to become lean and stay lean. I'll give you some suggestions to help you control your body fat and feel good about yourself.

It's desirable to be concerned about your level of body fat, but you get in trouble when your concern becomes an obsession and you're willing to use any means, no matter how extreme, to become lean. As you have learned from your hospitalization, extreme methods don't work, not for long anyway. I assure you that the best bodybuilding results, maximum muscle with minimum fat, come through moderation in both diet and exercise.

Starvation diets simply can't be sustained. You get hungry and feel so deprived that sooner or later you go on a binge. It's a feast or famine situation that gets you nowhere. (Starvation diets also bring about a loss of muscle tissue.)

It's neither advisable nor necessary to starve yourself. What you eat is more important than how much you eat. If you stick to a balanced diet of whole, unprocessed foods, you'll actually find it hard to overeat. Whole, natural foods are filling and satisfying, but low in calories. Avoid foods that have sugar or fat added and the fiber removed. Emphasize whole grains, fruits and vegetables in your diet, and be sure to eat some protein foods like milk and eggs. If you find it necessary to lose fat, cut back on your food intake *slightly* and increase your activity level *slightly*. Best results, especially long term, come from moderate, sustainable changes in how much you eat and exercise.

Weight training will protect and build lean muscle tissue while you're reducing your body fat, but don't go overboard with the weights either. For a beginner like you, I suggest three weight training sessions a week of about one hour each. Be sure to rest at least one day between training sessions.

You will find many more details in my books, *Ripped* and *Ripped 2*, but the main thing I want you to remember is that you can eat plenty of whole grains and bread, fruits and vegetables—all you can hold—without getting fat. Be sure to eat unprocessed foods with no sugar or fat added. Learn what kinds of food to eat, and you'll be able to eat your fill with no fear of getting fat.

CHAPTER TEN

HEALTH FACTORS

CHAPTER TEN: HEALTH FACTORS

Is It Healthy To Be Ripped?

Q. In your column in the November, 1980, issue, your advice on getting and staying ripped was excellent. But we both know that 12-15 percent body fat is necessary for good, adequate and steady response to day-to-day stress. Getting ripped is great as a goal for photo sessions, but it's not a healthy condition to maintain.

Your column is one of the best in this magazine, but please use it to promote a rational week-in, week-out program for health and fitness.

A. I'm often asked whether getting down to 2.4 percent body fat, as I have done repeatedly, is safe. Is it healthy? My answer is that it is safe and healthy, if you use a sensible approach to achieve ultimate muscularity.

Throughout 1980 I made a special effort to stay lean. I had Lovelace Medical Center measure my body composition periodically during the year, 10 times in all. My body fat slipped over four percent only twice. It was usually 3.1 percent. My high was 4.8 percent and my low was 2.7 percent.

Staying lean makes me look better but, more significantly, I feel better, too. I have no trouble responding to the stress I face every day in my law office. In fact, I'm more energetic. My wife points out that I walk faster and that I'm more active when I'm lean. I don't require as much sleep. My resting pulse rate is lower, in the low 50s. Simply put, I function better when I'm lean.

The 12-15 percent level that you recommend for good health is the average, normal fat level for young men. (At my age, 42, the average is about 22 percent.) I'm interested in achieving the "ideal," not the "average." *Muscle & Fitness* readers, like me, want to be better than average, a lot better. They want to be the best they can be.

Experiments have shown that about three percent is the limit below which a man can't reduce his fat without impairing normal body function and capacity for exercise. This three percent "essential fat" is in the marrow of your bones and in your heart, lungs, liver, spleen, kidneys, intestines, spinal cord and brain. The body will fight to protect its essential fat stores. Even during prolonged periods of starvation, the fat level in men doesn't drop much below three percent.

Many champion athletes have a low body fat level, very near the three percent essential fat level. Drs. Frank I. Katch and William D. McArdle, in their book *Nutrition, Weight Control and Exercise,* say that world-class male marathon runners range from about four to eight percent body fat. They measured the body composition of the New York Jets football team in the Human Performance Laboratory at Queens College in Flushing, New York. One three-time All-American linebacker had 3.1 percent body fat, and a defensive secondary player and an All-Pro offensive back both had four percent. Are these athletes unhealthy? Is their ability to deal with stress impaired? Katch and McArdle say their low fat content is a positive adaptation to prolonged, severe training.

In earlier times when food was scarce, body fat in excess of essential levels (storage fat) was important for survival. When food was plentiful our ancestors ate more than their energy expenditures required and added fat to their bodies. When food was in short supply, they used their stored body fat for fuel. Storage fat was a necessity. Fat cells filled up in good times and were emptied in hard times. The ups and downs balanced out and obesity was rare.

In modern times our cupboards are seldom bare. Junk food palaces threaten our waistlines at every turn. The famine never comes. We can get along just fine with our storage fat cells empty.

If you weigh 154 pounds and have 15 percent fat, you have 18.5 pounds of storage fat (plus 4.6 pounds of essential fat) or 65,000 calories of stored fuel. That's enough calories for you to live on for a month. No, I don't think you need 12-15 percent body fat to respond to normal day-to-day stresses.

I do, however, want to add some cautionary comments. With my body fat near essential levels most of the time, I am careful to eat regular meals. Many dieters brag that they don't eat breakfast or that they skip lunch. I try to never miss a meal. If I do, my energy level falls. I try to keep my calorie intake and my energy output in balance. When mealtime comes, my body tells me in no uncertain terms that it's time to eat. Regular meals keep my energy level on an even keel and I'm not tempted to overeat at the next meal. It may sound contradictory, but to get ripped and stay ripped, put food in your stomach regularly.

Finally, it's healthy to stay ripped only if you use healthy means to get ripped. If you follow an unhealthy diet to get ripped, then—for you—ripped will be unhealthy. It's undeniably true that many bodybuilders follow unhealthy, unbalanced diets to get into contest shape. They cut their carbohydrate intake to practically zero, and raise their protein intake sky-high. This type of diet places a tremendous strain on the body and makes you feel terrible. I know from personal experience that on this diet, normal everyday stresses can, indeed, be overwhelming. If you use an unhealthy, unbalanced diet to get in contest shape, the picture of health you present onstage will be a mirage.

To get ripped, follow a balanced diet of natural foods. And to stay ripped, stick with that diet. With a common sense approach, ripped looks healthy, feels healthy and is healthy.

NOTE:

It's extremely unlikely that you'll reduce your body fat so low that it's harmful to your health, but it is possible. According to a study reported in the *Journal of the American Medical Association,* the IRA hunger strikers probably died from depletion of their body fat.

Drs. Lawrence Leiter and Errol Marliss, of the departments of Medicine, University of Toronto and McGill in Canada, analyzed the data on the hunger strikers who died from fasting. The fasting men died after about 61 days of fasting; the range was 57 to 73 days. That's when they used up their body fat stores. Some bodybuilders go to extremes, but I don't think many would go that far. Personally, I never miss a meal.

Dr. Lawrence E. Lamb, writing in *The Health Letter* (April 8, 1983), points out another possible danger of being exceptionally thin: "Despite the advances in providing intravenous nutrition and support measures it is still true that individuals who must undergo periods of serious undernutrition need some body fat reserves to tide them through such emergencies."

Leanness and Life Span

Q. Aren't you afraid that maintaining such a low body fat level will shorten your life?

A. To the contrary, as I point out in *Ripped 2*, studies by Dr. Roy Walford, a pathologist and expert on aging at the UCLA School of Medicine, suggest that eating less may be the key to longer life. Animal studies by Dr. Walford and others indicate that a diet containing all the required nutrients but about a third fewer calories than needed to maintain "normal bodyweight" can add the equivalent of 40 years to a mammal's life. Comparable research has not been done on humans, but Dr. Walford believes the finding is applicable to people. "It works on every animal species thus far studied," he says.

In a recent letter to me, Dr. Walford confirmed the accuracy of my comments in *Ripped 2* about his studies. He went on to say, "I certainly agree with you that extreme leanness achieved through well-controlled diet can be healthy."

It's important to understand, however, that Dr. Walford doesn't advocate malnutrition as a means of extending life. It's healthy to be lean only if healthy means are used. If you follow an unhealthy diet to become lean, you'll probably be unhealthy. The unbalanced, starvation diets followed by some bodybuilders are unhealthy and aren't likely to have a positive effect on life span.

Exercise also seems to be an important factor in how long you live. In his recent letter Dr. Walford commented as follows: "In mouse studies, at least, there seems to be a relation between degree of dietary restriction and amount of exercise that is optimal for longevity. The greatest longevity is achieved in restricted animals who are moderately exercised, less in restricted animals who are heavily exercised, less still in normally fed animals who are heavily exercised, and shortest life span in normally fed animals who are not exercised."

Again, it appears that the key is moderation. Like extreme diets, extreme exercise programs may not be conducive to long life. But extreme leanness achieved through sensible diet and exercise may actually lead to a longer life.

If you're interested in exploring this subject further, I recommend Dr. Walford's book *Maximum Life Span* (W.W. Norton and Company, 1983).

Extreme leanness achieved through sensible diet and exercise may lead to longer life. *Photo by Bill Reynolds.*

Menstrual Irregularities

Q. Is it true that women bodybuilders with low body fat have irregular menstrual cycles? Is this harmful?

A. Menstrual irregularities were discussed at the Women's World Bodybuilding Championships held earlier this year (1981) in Atlantic City, New Jersey. It's true that many women athletes with body fat below 10 percent, women bodybuilders included, often experience menstrual irregularity. Some have an absence of menses for months or years. One of the contestants in Atlantic City confided to me that she was worried about the cessation of her menstrual cycle. She was afraid that her ability to become pregnant might be permanently impaired.

I researched this matter as soon as I returned home from Atlantic City. Fortunately, amenorrhea (complete absence of the menstrual cycle) as a result of exercise and low body fat is not permanent and does not indicate sterility. In 1979, the American College of Sports Medicine issued an "Opinion Statement on the Participation of the Female Athlete in Long Distance Running." It states emphatically: "Disruption of the menstrual cycle is a common problem for female athletes. While it is important to recognize this problem and discover its etiology, no evidence exists to indicate that this is harmful to the female reproductive system."

Dr. Ken Foreman, coach of the 1980 U.S. Olympic women's track and field team, is an exercise physiologist who has been studying amenorrhea for more than 10 years. In a personal conversation he told me, "There isn't one shred of evidence that amenorrhea in female athletes causes premature menopause."

Dr. Joan Ullyot, a physician specializing in sportsmedicine and a world-class marathoner herself, agrees. Her advice to women athletes with amenorrhea is: "Don't worry about it."

Cholesterol Controversy

Q. In a recent issue of *Muscle & Fitness* you described your current diet, which differs somewhat from the diet given in your book *Ripped*. For one thing, you seem to have dropped eggs? Are you worried about cholesterol?

A. The cholesterol scare has died down some in recent years, but many doctors still recommend that eggs, because of their high cholesterol content, be eaten only in limited quantities. This, however, isn't why I've reduced my egg consumption. As a matter of fact, when I was eating 18 eggs a day in 1978 my blood cholesterol level went down. Several years before that I tried to reduce my blood cholesterol by going on a low-cholesterol diet. My cholesterol went down for a while, but it soon returned to its previous level. It seems that if the diet doesn't provide enough cholesterol, the body manufactures more. Cholesterol is an essential biochemical in the body. When I reduced my dietary cholesterol, my body apparently compensated by producing more cholesterol.

Recently the medical establishment has decided that more important than the total cholesterol level is the ratio of high-density lipoproteins to low-density lipoproteins. If you have a high ratio of high-density lipoproteins, as I do, your risk of coronary heart disease is thought to be less. I don't know what the experts eventually will advise about cholesterol and, frankly, I've stopped worrying about it. Right now I'm more concerned about calories than cholesterol, and that's why I've reduced my egg consumption.

Eggs are high in fat, and fat contains more than twice the calories of carbohydrate and protein. One gram of fat has approximately nine calories, while one gram of protein or carbohydrate provides only four calories. I restrict my fat consumption to keep my caloric intake under control. I'm now more likely to have one egg for breakfast rather than the two or three I had in the past.

I also remove the cream from the milk I drink or make into yogurt. I rarely eat meat. I avoid butter, oil, gravy, et cetera. My emphasis on low-fat foods like grains, fruits and vegetables makes it easier for me to control my body fat. If my blood cholesterol level remains within reasonable limits in the bargain, it's an extra bonus.

I haven't made any basic change in my diet philosophy, but I'm constantly making adjustments to keep my calorie consumption and my energy expenditure in balance.

UPDATE:

Apparently the cholesterol controversy is finally over. A landmark 10-year study funded by the government at a cost of 150 million dollars has definitely demonstrated that lowering blood cholesterol, with diet and drugs, in men who have high levels can significantly reduce the likelihood of fatal and non-fatal heart attacks. In this study men who lowered their cholesterol 25 percent cut the incidence of heart disease by half. The researchers estimate that each one percent fall in cholesterol was associated with a two percent reduction in the rate of heart attacks. It clearly demonstrates that lowering blood cholesterol can decrease the risk of heart attacks, heart-disease-related deaths and other cardiovascular problems. The researchers believe that the study's findings also apply to women and to younger men with high blood cholesterol, particularly because heart disease is progressive and begins in youth.

Dr. Peter Wood, the science editor of *Runner's World* magazine, says the study clearly indicates that we all should increase our intake of vegetables, fruits and grains and decrease our intake of egg yolks, fatty meat, milk fat, butter and cheese. According to Dr. Wood, recent studies also show that running, cycling, brisk walking, cross-country skiing and other endurance sports result in increased levels of HDL cholesterol and often produce decreased levels of LDL cholesterol (the bad kind). Therefore, he also recommends regular aerobic exercise to decrease the risk of heart and circulatory problems.

Finally, Dr. Kenneth Cooper, in his latest book, *The Aerobics Program for Total Well-Being,* says, "Active people with low levels of body fat tend to show the best cholesterol balance in their blood" (high levels of HDL cholesterol in relation to total cholesterol). Cooper cites an evaluation of 900 prospective pilots performed by the American Airlines Medical Department over a three-year period. The study found that the pilots who were at or below their ideal weight had the lowest average cholesterol-to-HDL ratios.

The best and latest advice for most people seems to boil down to this: Eat less dietary fat, exercise more and maintain a low level of body fat. Clearly, we can chalk up another one for "the lean advantage."

Thyroid Pills

Q. I've lost 30 pounds and won four trophies over the last year and a half. I'm 38 years old but now I look like I'm 28. Still, I have a layer of fat around my stomach that never goes away. The guys at the gym where I train recommend that I get some thyroxine to speed up my thyroid gland. Will thyroxine get rid of the fat on my stomach?

A. Some bodybuilders use thyroid extract to speed up their metabolisms and help them burn body fat. I don't recommend it.

Thyroxine is a principal hormone produced by the thyroid gland. It does stimulate the rate of metabolism and help the body burn excess fat. The problem is that if your thyroid gland is functioning normally—as is true for the vast majority of people—taking thyroid hormone will at best speed up your metabolism only temporarily. Its presence causes your own gland to become lazy and cut back its hormone production. Then, after you stop taking thyroid, your natural hormone production will be below normal. This will cause you to have a tendency to gain fat. People who lose weight while taking thyroid pills almost always gain the weight back—usually in the form of fat—when they stop taking them.

Another problem is that weight lost while on thyroid medication includes muscle as well as fat. As a matter of fact, chronic overdosing on thyroid causes emaciation; you end up lean but with no muscle. Thyroid hormone may also cause heart irregularities, nervousness and insomnia.

In short, I think your gym buddies are giving you a bum steer.

Laxative Abuse

Q. How does a person who has become dependent on laxatives remedy this problem?

A. Your problem is a common one. Americans spend over $300 million a year on laxatives. More than 700 different laxative preparations are sold over the counter in this country. Many of these products stimulate the muscles of the colon and rectum, and repeated use can cause the bowel to lose the ability to function on its own. This type of laxative can also cause cramps, diarrhea and excessive loss of fluids and essential minerals.

First, I suggest that you switch to a bulk laxative. Your pharmacist can suggest one. This type of product increases the water content of the feces.

Experts like Denis Burkitt, M.D., author of *Eat Right—To Stay Healthy and Enjoy Life More* (ARCO, 1979), believe that lack of dietary fiber is the main reason constipation is common in the

Western world. Dietary fiber—from whole grains, fruits and vegetables—has a natural laxative effect. Like bulk laxatives, fiber absorbs water in the bowel, increases the volume of feces and speeds the movement of food through the intestinal tract. The long-term solution to your problem is probably a high-fiber diet of the kind I recommend in my books, *Ripped* and *Ripped 2*. A diet that relies heavily on whole grains, fruits and vegetables is not only the best way to lose fat and stay lean, it's also a first-rate cure for constipation.

I should warn you that it's best to switch to a high-fiber diet gradually. If you consume too much fiber too soon, it can cause bloating and gas. Another problem is that a high-fiber diet can interfere with the absorption of nutrients your body needs. Make the switch slowly so your digestive tract will have time to adjust.

CHAPTER ELEVEN

THE AGE
FACTOR

CHAPTER ELEVEN: THE AGE FACTOR

Motivation More Important Than Age

Q. If a bodybuilder continues to train with heavy weights after the age of 30, can he still maintain size? I've noticed that many of the top over-40 contestants are relatively slim and defined. I always thought that as long as you are willing to give up definition, you can maintain size. I admire the bulky type of physique, and the thought that bulk can't be maintained after 40 bothers me.

A. It's possible for a bodybuilder over 30, 40 and even 50 to maintain both size and definition. The main thing that seems to diminish with the years is the drive to train. I believe that with the proper mental attitude a bodybuilder can be as good in his 40s as he was in his 20s, or even better. Cases in point are Bill Pearl, Ed Corney, Jim Morris and Chris Dickerson.

You are correct, however, that many of the men in the Past-40 Mr. America contest are relatively slim and quite defined. Examples of this type are Cliff Ford and me. Kent Kuehn, the 1977 Past-40 Mr. America, and Phil Outlaw, the 1979 winner, are bigger and somewhat less defined.

As they get older, many men become more aware of the importance of overall fitness. This may be the reason many of the over-40 contestants are slim and defined rather than bulky.

In 1971, at the age of 41, Bill Pearl won the Mr. Universe title for the fourth time. He weighed 242 and was in the best shape of his career. Then, shifting the emphasis of his training to cardiovascular fitness, he reduced his body weight and added a lot of bicycling and running to his program. Later he went back to heavy bodybuilding, gained weight and, at 48, returned to top form for posing exhibitions at the 1978 Mr. America and Mr. Olympia contests. Bill is living proof that, with proper motivation, bodybuilders can and do maintain their size and definition into what, for most sports, is considered rocking chair time.

Stop worrying about what will happen to your size when you turn 40. Stay motivated, use your head, and keep training. You'll be better at 40 than you are now.

UPDATE:

Albert Beckles, who on February 25, 1984, won his second World's Professional Bodybuilding Championship, proves that training progress is more motivation than age. Beckles' age is something of a mystery, varying from article to article and magazine to magazine. However, the latest—from the July 1984 *Muscle & Fitness*—is that he's 52. Albert credits his continued improvement to genetics, regular training, proper diet and mental attitude—"You can go on as long as you want," he says.

Use It Or Lose It

Q. I'm 61 and my training partner is 55. We're motivated, consistent weight trainers. Should we follow the "no pain, no gain" philosophy of training or should we stick with light weights and take it easy?

A. Aging and taxes may be inevitable, but you don't have to treat them the same. As a lawyer I'd advise you to cooperate with the IRS. But aging is different. Fight it all the way.

Aging is as much mental as it is physical. Most people expect to decline physically when they reach 25—so they do. Professional football players expect their careers to be over at age 30; baseball players expect to be over the hill at 35. These expectations tend to become self-fulfilling prophecies.

At 41, Bill Pearl challenged every bodybuilder in the world to compete against him in the Mr. Universe contest. He believed he was the best, and he went on to win the title for the fourth time. Forty-one-year-old Chris Dickerson didn't let age keep him from winning the 1980 Grand Prix overall championship. In 1979, at age 41, I wrote in my book *Ripped* that "I have the best physique I've ever had." I also said, "I will be better in 1980." I was. Now I'm working hard to have an even better physique in 1981 than I had in 1980. I expect to succeed.

Time magazine recently quoted Dr. James Fries of the Stanford University Medical Center on the effect of exercise and positive thinking on the aging process. Dr. Fries said, "I tell patients to exercise—use it or lose it. 'Run, not rest' is the advice given by most cardiologists. The body is now felt to rust out rather than wear out."

Dr. Fries also pointed out that every organ has what is best described as a reserve capacity. "If loss of this reserve function represents aging, then exercising an organ represents a strategy for modifying the aging process." You and your training partner will develop and maintain a maximum reserve capacity only if you extend your body with heavy, hard training.

However, I'm not urging you to throw caution to the winds. A bodybuilder of any age should warm up properly and maintain strict form for each exercise. Jerking or throwing the weight makes any movement less effective and can cause injury. As you get older, it takes longer for injuries to heal. You and your training partner should pay particular attention to warm-up and exercise form.

You should also accept the fact that at your age it will take longer to recover and benefit from heavy training sessions. If your body hasn't recovered from a heavy training session, rest an extra day or substitute the hard workout you had planned with a light session or a long walk.

You and your training partner will make gains if you train hard and intelligently, and believe in yourselves. You'll be old only when you think you're old. Use it or lose it.

Exercise Slows Aging

Q. I haven't trained with weights for about 20 years, but I recently read your book, *Ripped,* and I'm hooked again. I'm 48 years old, five feet seven inches, and weigh 142 pounds. My present measurements are: arm 13½ inches, chest 41 inches, waist 34 inches, thighs 21 inches, calves 13½ inches. I've stayed fairly fit, but I've just recently started weight training again. At my age do you think I could possibly reach the following measurements: arms 16 inches, chest 44 inches, waist 32 inches, thighs 24 inches and calves 15 inches.

A. First, don't be too concerned about measurements. What really counts is the overall appearance of your physique.

Some years back an article in a muscle magazine about a bodybuilder would have been incomplete without measurements.

There's no better example of the effect of bodybuilding on aging than 53-year-old Bill Pearl. Bill has trained all his life and this is how he looked at the 1981 Professional Mr. Universe contest. *Photo courtesy of Bill Pearl.*

I served as a judge with Bill at the 1979 Southern Professional Cup held in Miami, Florida. I should ask Bill what exercise he recommends for the hairline. *Photo by Denie.*

Today you'll notice that measurements are rarely mentioned. The only two measurements I take are my body weight and my waist measurement. Even body weight doesn't mean anything unless you know how much is fat. The waist measurement helps in this regard, because an increase in your waist measurement almost always means a buildup of fat.

The best measuring tool is your mirror. If you rely too heavily on measurements you may be discouraged when you shouldn't be. It would be much better to keep track of your weight-training poundages. That will tell you whether you're building muscle. Your measurements may not change even though you're losing fat and adding muscle. Your weight-training poundages and the mirror, taken together, will tell you how you're doing.

There's no getting around the fact that age is a factor in bodybuilding success. But it isn't as much of a factor as we're generally led to believe. *Esquire* magazine recently carried a feature on the aging process. It was depressing and, to my way of thinking, a little misleading. The article states matter-of-factly that we lose about one percent of our functional capacity every year after age 30. The author suggests that our "best strategy may simply be to relax... and accept peacefully the indignities as they occur."

Sure, I know we're all aging, but I don't think we have to be ravaged to the extent the magazine article indicated. We can do more about it than simply watch in stupefied amazement.

We don't have to decline by 10 percent for each decade after age 30. Some of the best bodybuilders in the world—Chris Dickerson, Ed Corney, Bill Pearl and Serge Nubret, for example—didn't reach their peak until they were over 40. I look better now at 44 than I did when I was 34. I gained more than 10 pounds of muscle between the ages of 39 and 43. My cardiovascular fitness improved over the same period. In 1977, when I was 39, my oxygen uptake capacity was 50 percent above average. Last year, when I was 43, my uptake capacity increased slightly and I was found to be 55 percent above average.

Addressing the subject in his column in *Runner's World* magazine, Dr. George Sheehan says that what is generally taken for aging isn't really aging, it's "rusting." Sheehan says that the generally accepted 9-10 percent decline per decade is derived from misleading data based on people who've done nothing to stay young in function.

Sheehan is presently involved in a study designed to measure the physiological decline in athletes who continue to train and attempt to perform up to their potential. The rate of deterioration for this group is only about five percent per decade, half the usually quoted rate. In support of this figure, Sheehan points out that the world marathon record for 40-year-olds is within five percent of the world record. Sheehan himself, at over 60, can still run the mile in 5 minutes and 10 seconds, only 20 percent slower than his best college time of 4:20.

I'm going to do my best to get better over the next few years. I see no reason why you shouldn't do the same. As Dr. Sheehan says, "go for it!"

UPDATE:

John A. Kelley, a 76-year-old marathoner, is a wonderful example of the effect of exercise on aging. Kelley, who just ran his 53rd Boston Marathon—he's completed 111 marathons and won Boston twice—was tested at Dr. Kenneth Cooper's Aerobics Center in Dallas.

Dr. Cooper was excited to evaluate Kelley because, with only a few exceptions, since the age of 16 he's run every day of his life. He still runs hard, an hour or more seven days a week and up to two-and-one-half hours before an important race. He told Jim Fixx, who wrote up the test results for *The Runner* magazine, "When I run a race, I'm out for blood. I want to do my best."

On the treadmill test, perhaps the single most reliable indicator of an individual's condition, Kelley lasted 24 minutes. This put him in the "excellent" category for men aged 39-and-under and in the "superior" category for men over 40. By comparison, a well-conditioned and forty-years-younger Roger Staubach lasted 30 minutes.

Johnny's overall physical condition—he's a trim 135 pounds at five feet five inches with a blood pressure of 110/78 and a resting heart rate of 52—is comparable to that of the top four percent of men 40 to 49 years old. "We're looking at a man 25 to 30 years younger than his chronological age," Cooper told Fixx. "Even allowing for good genes, it's my guess that it's exercise that has kept him young."

George Sheehan, who I refer to and quote above, recently turned 65 and took the opportunity to provide further evidence of the

192

payoff from exercise. After a 20-year layoff to establish his medical practice, Sheehan started running again in his early 40s. He's been running ever since, at distances up to the marathon.

Tested at the Cooper Clinic along with John Kelley, Sheehan established a new 65-and-over record on the treadmill. As with Kelley, Dr. Cooper steadily increased the grade—and after 25 minutes the speed—of the treadmill until Sheehan couldn't go any further: 28 minutes and 30 seconds. In addition to being a record for his age, Dr. Sheehan's performance put him in the "superior" category for men under 30—the elite category for men of all ages.

Sheehan, a cardiologist, claims when he dies they'll have to beat his heart to death with a stick. Maybe it's true.

Goals For Mature Bodybuilders

Q. I'm 39 years old. When I started working out two years ago I had no involvement in sports and was underdeveloped. Although I have achieved my primary goal of losing weight and am stronger than I was at 18, now I would like to concentrate on real muscular development. What are realistic goals for a mature man?

A. If you are in good health and motivated, your goals don't have to be any different than those of a teenager or young adult. At 45 my goal is the same as it was at 18: to get better. The swelling ranks of mature men presently involved in vigorous physical activity are proving that age is not a major stumbling block to high-level athletic performance. Your bodybuilding success will be more a function of how hard you train than of your age. If you remain motivated and injury-free, you can become almost as muscular at 40 as you could have at 20.

A case in point is powerlifter Jim Lem. Lem didn't start to compete in powerlifting until he was about your age. He competed in his first contest in 1970 after lifting weights for only three years. He is now 53 years old and still improving. He holds 11 world records in the 50 to 59 age division. He also holds the northern California records in the squat and deadlift in the 181-pound division at 667 and 634 respectively.

Lem was recently featured on the cover of *Powerlifting USA* magazine; he was quoted inside as saying, "The best is yet to come." He's shooting for a 700-pound squat!

Lem is not an isolated case. Dr. Michael L. Pollock of the Human Performance Laboratory at Mount Sinai Medical Center in Milwaukee, Wisconsin, has been studying a group of 24 master runners for more than a decade. All were 40 or over and considered champions at the beginning of the study. Dr. Pollock found that those who continued to exercise aggressively actually improved over the decade. Training intensity seemed to be the key. All 24 continued to train, but only those who continued to train hard maintained or improved their fitness level.

Another of Dr. Pollock's findings is of special interest to bodybuilders. The runners who used weights in their training were able to maintain their lean body mass and showed no increase in body fat. Those who did not use weights lost muscle mass.

Muscle After 45?

Q. I'm 42 and have been training with weights for six months. My goal is to become as lean and muscular as I can. I guess I'll have to get the job done in three years, because I've heard that 45 is the cutoff point for building muscle. Is that true?

A. No. You can build muscle at any age; it's just harder when you're older. Testosterone, the hormone that allows men to build bigger muscles than women, slowly declines with age. When you're older, your capacity to recover from training is also somewhat less.

In a sense, the fact that you're starting to train late in life is an advantage. You haven't tapped your potential for building muscle. You have what I call a "virgin body." Like any other beginner, your body will respond readily to weight training. Any resistance beyond what you're used to will make your muscles grow. You have nowhere to go but up.

The effect of age on the ability to build muscle is gradual, and your muscle-building capacity won't stop dead at 45. David L. Costill, Ph.D., director of the Human Performance Laboratory at Ball State University in Muncie, Indiana, is probably the best known exercise physiologist in America, if not the world. In an interview in *The Runner* magazine, Dr. Costill said: "The body is capable of adaptation, and as you get older, you don't necessarily go down the tubes. Probably when you reach about 65 you go down, even with training, but you still stay higher than if you don't train."

These photos show my improvement between age 39 and 45. In 1977, when I was 39, I was already hard and muscular with 2.4 percent body fat, but I was much better in 1983 at 45—one percent body fat and 11 pounds more muscle. *Photos by Dave Sauer (1977) and Guy Appelman (1983).*

So you probably have at least 20 good bodybuilding years ahead of you.

In the same interview, Costill cautioned that we deteriorate rapidly unless we keep training. If you stop bodybuilding when you turn 45, it won't be long before your gains disappear. It will be as if you never trained. You made the right decision six months ago and should plan to continue training indefinitely.

Few, if any, studies have been done on the capacity of older strength athletes, but older endurance athletes have been compared to young athletes. Dr. George Sheehan, a master's runner, in his "Running Wild" column in *The Physician and Sportsmedicine* magazine, told the results of such a study. He was a participant. Sheehan's master's group (age 53-65) were compared with 16 young athletes to whom they were matched on the basis of training regimens, and to 18 untrained middle-aged men. The master's athletes were found to have oxygen uptakes 20-30 percent greater than those of the sedentary younger men. Based on a comparison with their younger running counterparts, it was estimated that the master's athletes had declined only 5 percent per decade rather than the 9 percent per decade usually seen in men over 25. Sheehan concluded, "And we had an average VO_2 max 50 percent higher than former champion runners our age who had not trained for 20 or more years."

My guess is that such a comparison for older bodybuilders would produce similar results. If you train with weights now and continue to train as you get older, you'll have more muscle mass than younger men who don't train and, compared to untrained men your age, you'll be a muscular marvel.

What's more, you'll have an important advantage when you're 45—the advantage of three years of training experience. Experience allows a person to get more out of training. I proved that this year.

I first achieved a 2.4 percent body fat level in 1977, and I've reduced my body fat to that level a number of times since then. But in spite of repeated efforts, I wasn't able to reduce my body fat any lower.

In 1983, I finally succeeded in getting leaner than ever before. On August 26, 1983, Lovelace Medical Foundation, Research Division, measured my body fat level at one percent. And significantly, I hit one percent body fat at my highest lean bodyweight. This time my body didn't rebel and sacrifice muscle. I actually increased my muscle mass as I reduced below 2.4 percent fat. The Lovelace research staff found that, compared to 1977 when I first reached 2.4 percent body fat, when I hit one percent fat my lean muscle mass was 11 pounds higher.

Age hasn't increased my muscle-building capacity, but my years of training experience have taught me more about how to gain muscle while losing fat. I'm sure experience will help you in a similar way.

And finally, you can be sure of one thing: If you think you can't build muscle after 45, you won't.

CHAPTER TWELVE

YOUNG BODYBUILDERS

CHAPTER TWELVE: YOUNG BODYBUILDERS

Weight Training For Teens

Q. I would appreciate your opinion on my 14½-year-old son working out. He's five feet, four inches and weighs 104, which is relatively small for his age. Would working out be detrimental to his growth and development?

A. Weight training was one of the most positive things I did as a teenager. I started training off and on when I was about 12 and was training regularly when I was your son's age. Weight training quickly taught me that working at something conscientiously really pays off. It enhanced my self-image tremendously.

I'm sure weight training will help your son both physically and emotionally, especially since he's small for his age and may be self-conscious about it.

It's important that weight training be fun for a youngster. Encourage him to train, but don't push him. He doesn't need to lift heavy weights, but should work on doing the exercises properly and getting a feel for how his muscles work. Have him stick with basic exercises for 10 repetitions or more. My father always encouraged me to weight train, but he never pressured me. You should do the same for your son. Make it a fun father-son activity.

You should also help your son develop an appreciation of good nutrition. Right now he is at a critical stage from the standpoint of fat-cell development. The number of fat cells increases three times during a person's life: in the last three months before birth, in the year after birth, and during the adolescent growth spurt. (The total number of fat cells doesn't increase during adulthood.) The number of fat cells developed during these critical periods determines, in part, whether you'll have a tendency to be fat as an adult. In other words, if you're fat as a child, you're likely to be fat as an adult. In their book, *Nutrition, Weight Control and Exercise,* body-composition experts Frank I. Katch and William D. McArdle

This is how I looked at 15, shortly after I began lifting weights. Training had a very positive effect on my development.

advise: "Early prevention of obesity through exercise and diet, rather than correction of existing obesity, may be the most effective way to curb the grossly-overfat condition so common in adults."

My weight training made me conscious of diet and nutrition when I was a teenager. Weight training and a good diet then kept me lean and laid the groundwork for me to become a lean adult. I can't think of anything that you could do for your son that would be more constructive than to encourage him to train with weights and eat sensibly.

NOTE:

The American Academy of Pediatrics (AAP) is opposed to lifting maximum poundages until the skeleton is essentially mature, which occurs about age 16 or 17. The reason is that heavy weights might damage the cartilaginous growth centers present in immature bones. The AAP supports weight training for youngsters using weights well below maximum, however. Straining against maximum poundages—as in competitive Olympic lifting and

Power lifting—should be delayed until the cartilage in the bones hardens into mature bone.

As I said, young bodybuilders don't need to use heavy weights; they should concentrate on doing the exercises properly and get a feel for how the muscles work. In any event, weight training before puberty, when the testicles start releasing testosterone—the male hormone which stimulates muscular development—won't produce optimum results, at least in building muscles.

For youngsters, the best advice is "train, but don't strain."

Advice To A Young Fanatic

Q. I'm 15 years old and have been bodybuilding for over three years. I've overtrained excessively in the past, sometimes spending up to 12 hours a day (about four lifting), six-seven days a week on athletic work. I pushed at least half of my hundreds of sets weekly to failure. I recently have turned to mega-intensity training but, by habit, have even overtrained on this. I've lost much weight in the past and gained it back by eating unwisely. In the last six months I became a fanatic about food, too, eating as little as 1200 calories daily and cutting out even slightly harmful foods.

I've finally got my act somewhat together and am training a little less and eating more sensibly. Any help you can give me would be greatly appreciated.

A. Like you, I once would have eaten almost anything and trained all day if I thought it would make me bigger and stronger. Frankly, I'm still willing to do just about anything that will make me a better bodybuilder, but my years of training have taught me some things that I think will help you.

Extreme diets and training methods are usually not the most productive. A program of brief, intense weight training combined with a moderate amount of aerobic exercise, adequate rest and a well-balanced diet gives the best results.

I've also learned that it's a mistake to devote yourself to bodybuilding to the extent that other important aspects of life— school, job, family, et cetera—are neglected. It's a mistake because it makes you an unbalanced individual, but also because it's not necessary. You don't have to neglect your other obligations to train properly. I trained hard all through law school. In fact, I made lifetime records in the Olympic lifts during the final exam week of my second year of law school and, at the same time, ranked number one in my class. I understand your enthusiasm for bodybuilding, but don't let bodybuilding interfere with your school work. If you apply yourself, you can do both well.

I gather from your letter that your bodybuilding experience hasn't always been pleasant. Bodybuilding should be enjoyed, not suffered, and you probably won't continue training unless you enjoy it. Leo Buscaglia, the famous writer and speaker on living and loving successfully, says, "All paths are the same. They lead nowhere." Dr. Buscaglia says this not to discourage enthusiasts like you and me, but to remind us that we should find enjoyment in our day-to-day activities. George Sheehan, the famous doctor-runner-writer-philosopher, phrases it a little differently. He says, "Happiness, we come to discover, is found in the pursuit of happiness." Your training is a means to an end, but you should savor every workout. The pleasure of bodybuilding comes not only from developing a good physique, but also from the process of getting there.

Last weekend I observed a weight-training coach who puts this philosophy into practice. My friend Carl Miller invited me to Santa Fe, New Mexico, to be a judge at an Olympic-style weightlifting meet he sponsored at his new Santa Fe Sports Medicine Center. The competitors were mostly young, novice lifters of average ability. Nevertheless, Carl highlighted each lifter's accomplishment. It made no difference how much weight was on the bar; Carl was just as enthusiastic about a 100-pound personal record as he was about a new state record. Even when a lifter failed, he praised the effort. For Carl, the important thing wasn't how a lift ranked *vis-a-vis* state, national or world records, but whether it was a good effort for the individual lifter. Carl made all the competitors feel like champs. Because of Carl, they all enjoyed the process of lifting.

I urge you to do the same. Train in a way that you enjoy, and it will make no difference whether you become a world champion or only the best-built person on your block; it will all be worthwhile.

Starting With A Boom

Q. I'm 14¾ years old and I've been lifting weights since I was

204

13½. I started bodybuilding because I've always been picked on in school, harassed, et cetera.

On September 30, 1981, I had just gotten to school and went to my locker when someone tapped me on the shoulder. I turned around and "boom" this kid hit me right in the nose. Blood gushed. I went to the hospital and had to have x-rays. The doctor said I was lucky my nose wasn't broken.

So then, I built up enough confidence and went right back to school the next day (boy was I scared). As I was walking to school a whole group of boys in my grade were standing out in front of the school waiting for me. When I got there I knew something was wrong, almost every boy in my grade was out there. When I got to my first class not a single one of the students could believe I was back the next day.

That weekend, I thought this has to be the end of all the teasing and hitting. So I started bodybuilding. After two months had passed we had bodybuilding in our PE class. The boy who hit me was in the class. Boy did I scare him off. I was the strongest person in the class. He just couldn't believe it. After that he was trying to be friends with me and stay on my good side.

This year in bodybuilding at school I was the strongest in class. I outlifted the freshmen in my class and the sophomores and juniors, too. I squatted 230 pounds, cleaned 145 and bench pressed 145. Everyone in class called me "Muscles" and "Animal." This all took place last month.

A. I hope you don't mind my sharing your story with the readers of *Muscle & Fitness*. I loved hearing how you got started in bodybuilding. Keep up the good work.

CHAPTER THIRTEEN

TRAINING FOR OTHER SPORTS

CHAPTER THIRTEEN: TRAINING FOR OTHER SPORTS

Getting Ripped For Cycling

Q. I have just started a weight training program to improve my performance in my favorite sport, cycling. I don't want to develop a Mr. America physique. Instead, I want to get down to optimum cycling weight (about 165 for me) and develop the muscles that help me push the pedals and win.

A. You've got the right idea. With the exception of activities like Sumo wrestling, where great bulk is an advantage, getting lean and hard—"ripped" in bodybuilding language—will improve your performance in almost any sport. Excess fat impairs efficiency in everything you do from mowing the lawn to running a marathon.

I'm an avid cyclist myself and have put many miles on my 10-speed. I know that I can ride farther and faster when I'm very lean. This past year I concentrated on training for a physique competition and didn't ride my bike for months. When I started cycling again after the contest I found I could spin up the hills just about as fast as when I was riding regularly. Bodybuilding kept me in good cardiovascular shape and also strengthened the muscles used in cycling.

You are correct, however, that weight training can be used most effectively to improve performance in another sport if you concentrate on the specific muscles involved in that sport. Twenty-inch arms won't help a cyclist; they'd be excess baggage and would simply weigh you down on the flats and hills.

To bring your weight down to an efficient 165 pounds, follow a balanced, low-calorie diet. To build strength to improve your cycling, but avoid adding muscle mass that would hamper your performance, focus your weight training on the lower back, hips, thighs and calves. Work the rest of your body just enough to maintain muscle tone. Don't worry about building muscle where you don't want it. Rest assured, muscles you don't work hard won't grow.

I've been biking since the mid-sixties, and I can definitely ride farther and faster when I'm very lean. *Photo by Bill Reynolds.*

Golfer Wants Strength and Flexibility

Q. I'm a 34-year-old woman golfer with an eight handicap. I've won city and club golfing championships and rank 25th in my state. I need added strength and flexibility in my golfing muscles. My biggest problem is not turning my hips enough on the backswing. I also need more strength and flexibility in my right forearm. I'm interested in a training routine specifically for golf muscles, but I'm also concerned that developing my muscles might hamper my game. I would appreciate your advice.

A. I'm sure a well-designed weight-training program will help your golf.

Progressive resistance exercise done through a full range of motion will make you stronger and will develop your speed and flexibility. Because a woman has fewer androgenic hormones than a man, she cannot develop the muscle size and strength of a man, but she definitely can become much stronger through weight training.

Don't worry about muscular development hurting your golf game. Some of the most muscular men are also the most flexible. John Grimek, one of the most muscular men in history, could touch both elbows to the floor from a standing position without bending his knees, and could do full splits with ease.

Frank Stranahan, a top pro golfer of a few years ago, was an avid weight lifter. He could clean and jerk 300 pounds, squat with 400, and deadlift 500, all at the time he was playing his best golf. He gave weight training a lot of credit for his outstanding golf game.

Weight training can increase your flexibility if you do the exercises slowly through a full range of motion, with a good stretch at the beginning and a full contraction at the end. Muscles not used through their full range of motion lose flexibility. Weight training is the best way to load your muscles through their full range of motion and, therefore, maintain and increase flexibility.

Don't limit your weight-training routine to your problem areas. You'll get best results from a balanced, overall routine. When you strengthen one set of muscles, it's important that you also strengthen the opposite set. For example, you should work your hamstrings along with your quadriceps. A golfer will benefit from added strength and flexibility in the legs, hips, back, chest, shoulders and arms—the entire body. Focus on your hips and forearms, which you say are your problem areas, but work your entire body at the same time.

Don't make the mistake of thinking that light weights are better than heavy weights for a golfer. It takes heavy weights to develop strength, and only with heavy weights can you force your body into the fullest possible range of motion. Full-range, heavy exercises will help you the most.

You can also benefit from stretching exercises. Again, use a complete program. Don't limit your stretching to one or two areas. Spend time on your special needs, but do it in the context of a complete stretching program. Stretching exercises should be performed smoothly. Don't bounce. Be careful not to force the stretch beyond your tolerance. An excellent book on stretching which includes a section for golfers is *Stretching* by Bob Anderson (Shelter Publications, Inc. 1980).

A final factor to consider is your body fat level. Excess body fat limits your range of motion and, therefore, your power and speed. A balanced, low-calorie diet plus aerobic exercise is the best way to lose fat. Your weight-training program will allow you to maintain and increase your muscle mass while you reduce your body fat to an optimum level.

A full-range, heavy weight-training program for your entire body, plus stretching and body fat reduction, will make you a better golfer. So pump iron to swing your irons better.

CHAPTER FOURTEEN

SPECIAL PROBLEMS

CHAPTER FOURTEEN: SPECIAL PROBLEMS

Loose Skin

Q. I'm obsessed with a desire to build a "winning body." However, my loose skin stands in the way of my getting ripped.

A. I receive a surprising number of letters asking how to get rid of loose skin. I've never had this problem because I've always trained and been careful about keeping my weight down. If you let the pounds pile on and then reduce, it takes time for the skin to adjust and tighten up. This is particularly true if you lose weight quickly and without exercise. Experiments have shown that when an overweight person reduces by fasting, up to 66 percent of the weight loss is lean tissue. And loss of lean tissue is likely to cause loose skin. By losing gradually and exercising regularly, lean tissue is maintained and loose skin is minimized.

The loose skin problem is compounded by the "yo-yo syndrome"—repeatedly going on a crash diet, losing weight, and then gaining the weight back a short time later. Covert Bailey described the situation in his book, *Fit or Fat?* He wrote, "The American public has been on a diet for 25 years—and has gained five pounds." Each time the yo-yo cycle is repeated, more lean tissue is lost and more loose skin results.

If you have loose skin the solution is to become lean through sensible diet and exercise. Then stay lean so your skin will adjust and tighten up. Don't kid yourself, however. Be sure that your problem is loose skin and not a layer of fat underneath your skin. You have fat to lose if you can pinch more than one-half inch of skin on your waistline.

More About Loose Skin

Q. I have a problem with loose, sagging skin on the inside of my thighs as a result of a big weight loss. I started my diet weighing 417

To prevent loose skin, it's important to exercise and keep your weight under control. *Photo by Wayne Gallasch.*

Photo by Guy Appelman.

pounds and currently weigh 197. I've maintained my weight loss for eight years.

I'm a construction worker, now working as a supervisor. I don't get as much exercise as I used to. I had an operation for loose skin on my stomach. Is there anything short of surgery I can do for the loose skin on my thighs?

A. Loose skin frequently occurs after a large weight loss. A number of things can be done to avoid or eliminate the problem, but sometimes it's so severe that surgery is the only answer.

Ken Passariello, the 1981 light-weight world bodybuilding champion, reduced from a pudgy 250 pounds to a rock-hard 154. He reduced his body fat from approximately 50 percent to an incredible 1.8 percent. Ken has some stretch marks on his lower abdomen, but otherwise shows no signs of his former corpulence. Bruce Randall, who won the Mr. Universe title a number of years ago, had a weight loss similar to yours; he reduced from over 400 pounds to under 200. He showed no signs of the fact that his skin had been stretched to an extreme degree when he was heavy. At the 1982 Jr. Mr. USA contest in Memphis, Tennessee, one of the Over-40 competitors (who also did well in the open competition) had reduced his bodyweight by almost 100 pounds. Although he has developed an outstanding physique, he still has loose skin in his abdominal area. I discussed this with him after the contest, and he said his doctor told him surgery was the only solution.

Age may be a factor in whether skin tightens up after a large weight loss. Youth probably helped Passariello and Randall overcome the problem, but age may have worked against the competitor I talked to in Tennessee. How long a person remains heavy may also bear on whether the skin will tighten up after weight reduction. I know that Randall was heavy for only a short time, and I believe this is also true of Passariello. Skin that has been stretched for many years simply isn't as resilient as skin stretched for only a short time.

I discussed your specific problem with my doctor. He tells me that in most cases the skin tightens up if the weight loss is maintained. Repeated weight gains and reductions aggravate the problem. In a case like yours, where the weight reduction has been maintained for eight years and sagging skin persists, my doctor tells me that surgery is probably the only answer. Nevertheless, I believe there are some things you can do that will help.

The fact that you're not exercising makes your problem worse. When exercise doesn't accompany weight loss, muscle tissue is lost, causing the skin to sag. The muscle that supports the skin comes off along with the fat. The same thing happens when a person becomes less active, as is the case with you. Even though you maintained your new low weight, when you cut down your activity, you may have lost muscle and gained fat. A regular weight-training program along with a well-balanced diet will help you gain muscle and lose fat. Replacing fat with muscle will help alleviate your problem by rebuilding the support structure under your skin.

Rapid weight loss can also cause loose skin. When you take the pounds off fast, your skin has less time to adjust. Furthermore, with the type of starvation diet necessary for rapid loss, the weight lost usually is about 75 percent muscle and water, and only 25 percent fat. Because supporting muscle tissue is lost, the result is loose skin. To avoid loose skin, it's important to reduce slowly; one or two pounds a week is a desirable rate.

Weight training will alleviate your problem somewhat but, as my doctor points out, additionally surgery will probably also be required.

People who want to avoid this problem should lose weight slowly, lift weights while reducing and keep the weight off when the goal is reached.

Body Hair

Q. What method do you use for removing body hair? I have a lot of hair on my chest, back, and shoulders. When I tried electrolysis, 80 percent of the hair grew back. Is there some kind of lotion that will remove hair?

A. The only area where I have permanently rid myself of hair is on the top of my head and that wasn't intentional. I don't know of any way to permanently remove body hair and I don't know if I would recommend it if I did.

The only time I remove my body hair is in preparation for a photo session or a contest. I find shaving with a dry safety razor works best. I've tried using shaving cream but it prevents me from seeing what I'm doing and I end up cutting myself. A dry blade also shaves quicker than a wet one. This may sound unusual since a wet blade and shaving cream are used to remove facial hair. But I'm sure you'll find shaving with a dry blade is the best way to remove body hair.

CHAPTER FIFTEEN

THE LEAN LIFESTYLE

CHAPTER FIFTEEN: THE LEAN LIFESTYLE

A Nation Of Fatties

Q. The episode of the television program *Nova* called "Fat Chance in a Thin World" has made me depressed. It was a program about the latest scientific findings on what makes people fat. The basic message was that diets don't work: 95 percent of those who lose weight gain it back within one year. By mid-life, more than half of Americans are overweight. What's more, *Nova* said it's getting worse: In the past 15 years, the weight of the average adult has increased by five pounds.

According to scientists on the program, the evidence is strong that there is genetic predisposition for obesity. Apparently obese people have abnormal fat cells and slow metabolism, which causes them to be overweight. Many fat people actually eat less than lean people. They have to literally starve themselves to achieve normal bodyweight. They seem to be programmed from birth to be overweight. The program painted a bleak picture. I've been fighting a weight problem all my life. Should I accept the fact that I was born to be fat and give up?

A. There's no question that we're a nation of fatties. Anybody can see that by observing people on the street. Nevertheless, I don't think you should throw in the towel. *Nova* mentioned two factors that convince me that most people can conquer the overweight problem.

Nova pointed out that there has been a strong shift in the American diet away from grains and vegetables, and towards meats and fats. The narrator said that studies with animals have found that obesity is not a natural phenomenon. Animals that live in the wild and eat the foods they've always eaten are rarely fat. I think the American weight problem is caused less by genetic factors than by the type of food we eat.

The other note of hope that came through was the role of exercise

My wife, Carol, and I enjoy our work at Ripped Enterprises—helping people adopt a lean lifestyle. *Photo by Wayne Gallasch.*

in weight control. The narrator made it clear that the benefit of exercise is greater than just the calories burned off by the activity. Dieting slows down your metabolism so that you gain weight faster when you get off the diet. Exercise counters this problem by speeding up your metabolism and helping you to lose weight and keep it off.

Years ago, when I first started reading books on weight control, the accepted notion was that diet was the only answer; that exercise wasn't a practical solution, because it takes 35 miles of running to run off a pound of fat. More recently, books like *The Dieter's Dilemma* by William Bennett, M.D. and Joel Gurin have taken the position that exercise is the only answer. Programs like *Nova* and Geneen Roth's book, *Feeding the Hungry Heart,* suggest that the answer may lie in accepting the fact that you weren't born to live up to the American ideal of thinness. I don't buy any of these extremes. With few exceptions, overweight conditions can be cured permanently through diet and exercise.

Over the years I've tried all the diets, and without question the best approach is to eat whole, unprocessed foods that are filling and satisfying but low in calories. Emphasize high-fiber foods (whole grains, fruits and vegetables). Most people can eat all they want of this type of food and not get fat. Avoid foods that have the fiber and bulk removed, and sugar or fat added.

I've always exercised, but it wasn't until I read Covert Bailey's book *Fit or Fat?* that I came to truly appreciate the role of exercise in weight control. As the narrator on *Nova* said, exercise speeds up your metabolism, both during the activity and after. (It also increases your fat burning capacity.) Regular exercise helps, even if we ignore its effect on basal metabolic rate. Simply walking two miles a day in a year's time will burn off 20 pounds of fat.

In addition to my books *Ripped* and *Ripped 2,* I recommend that you read two other books that explain how sensible diet combined with exercise will solve your weight problem: *The 200 Calorie Solution* by Martin Katahn, Ph.D. (Berkely Books, 1983) and *California Diet and Exercise Program* by Dr. Peter Wood (Anderson World Books, Inc., 1983). Both books are available from Ripped Enterprises.

So don't despair. I'm convinced that Americans are fat because of the kind of food we eat and because of our sedentary lifestyle; not because we're born to be fat.

I'm convinced that Americans are fat because of the kind of food we eat and because of our lifestyle. *Photo by Bill Reynolds.*

Lifetime Leanness

Q. A number of top bodybuilders who are ripped to the bone at contest time gain a tremendous amount of weight soon afterwards. Several weeks later you wouldn't believe the individual is the same person. I'd like to get lean and hard and stay that way. What's the best method?

A. I've experimented with all kinds of diets. The phenomenon you describe is a matter of physiological and psychological deprivation. These men go on very restricted diets that make them feel unsatisfied and create tremendous cravings for all the foods they deny themselves before a contest. Many bodybuilders live on fish, chicken, and water or coffee to get ripped. This type of diet inevitably leads to an eating binge after the contest. It's unhealthy, and certainly not the way to lifetime leanness.

There isn't space here for a dissertation on all aspects of getting ripped, but from my own experience I can give you the key to getting lean and staying lean. Stay away from crash diets of all kinds. They don't work on a long-term basis. Stick to a balanced diet of whole, unprocessed foods and don't rush the reducing process. Take your time in reducing and when you reach your desired weight you'll be able to stay there. Plan your diet around the four basic food groups: fruit and vegetables, whole grains, meat and eggs, and dairy products. Don't deny yourself food from any of the four basic groups, but—this is important—go easy on anything that has sugar or fat added, or the natural fiber and bulk removed. If you eat a variety of natural foods that have had nothing added or subtracted, you'll never feel hungry or deprived and you'll be lean for life.

I should add that it's difficult to maintain maximum leanness. To get truly ripped, you'll have to adhere to some additional rules and zero in with extra determination. But if you follow the basic rules I've given you, you'll be physiologically and psychologically content, and you'll be able to stay lean and hard continuously.

Tips For Out-Of-Fit Physician

Q. I'm a 42-year-old male physician and I lead a rather sedentary life. I have always enjoyed backpacking, rock climbing, skiing and racquetball, but lately I have had increasing difficulty doing these

Whole grains, fruits and vegetables can help you stay lean. *Photo by Guy Appelman.*

activities.

Last week at the Cooper Aerobics Clinic in Dallas I scored solidly in the "poor" category on the cardiorespiratory fitness test and my body fat measured a disastrous 24 percent.

I would like to improve my fitness and reduce my body fat. I would appreciate your advice regarding a diet and exercise program.

A. Doctors, lawyers and other professional and business people are often so busy solving problems of others that they neglect themselves. The results of your body composition and cardiorespiratory fitness tests have, apparently, convinced you that you should devote some time to yourself. You've been motivated to reduce your body fat and improve your aerobic fitness. Here are some tips, based on my own experience, that will make it easier and less time consuming for you to reach these goals.

First, read my "Ripped" department in the June, 1981, issue of *Muscle & Fitness.* (It's in Chapter Two of this book, "Diet to Stay Lean.") It provides a good summary of the diet I use to stay lean. Your diet should include a great deal of whole, natural foods that have all the bulk and fiber left in them and no sugar or fat added. You should eat plenty of whole grains, fruits and vegetables. Switching to this pattern of eating with no other changes will go a long way to help reduce your body fat.

Two simple techniques complement this diet and help you eat less: 1) eat slowly and 2) don't put more food on the table than you plan to eat.

You will eat less if you eat slowly because your stomach has enough time to signal your brain that you are full. However, it's not necessary to chew one mouthful numerous times, nor is it necessary to put your fork down between bites. Simply make it a point to take your time eating.

It helps to include something with each meal that must be chewed for a long time. For example, it takes longer to eat whole grain, cooked cereal than cornflakes. A large, raw carrot takes longer to chew than canned vegetables. Try this technique. It really works.

Take a few moments before each meal to plan what you're going to eat. And put only that food on the table. Extra portions tempt you to eat more. If you want more, you should have to get up from the table to get it. This makes you think twice about eating more and should make it easier to stick to your meal plan.

It's a good idea to keep high-calorie "goodies" out of the house. Once again, if the food isn't available, you won't eat it. Ask your family to help you with this. My wife and nine-year-old son try to keep high-calorie food out of my reach and sight.

Exercise is the other half of your fitness equation. A regular program of exercise will burn calories, build lean tissue and improve your aerobic fitness.

With a little planning you can make exercise part of your daily activity. And you won't have to take time to go to the gym or change clothes. For example, my office is on the third floor and I never take the elevator. I always use the stairs. This requires no extra time and, in the course of a year, it burns a lot of calories and fat. You can put similar practices into your daily routine. For example, when you're seeing patients at the hospital, use the stairs instead of the elevator. And try standing up when you talk on the telephone.

Of course, there's no need to overdo this. Don't make yourself uncomfortable. Over time, slight changes in your daily routine go a long way in helping you become leaner and more fit.

Your formal exercise program can be short and simple. Walking is an excellent way to burn calories and increase aerobic fitness. My wife and I walk three miles each morning before breakfast. The walk takes us less than an hour and it's a pleasant way to start the day. This may not be convenient for you, but I suggest that you look over your schedule and see if you can find some time for a brisk walk. What about 30 minutes right after lunch?

Walking on a regular basis is probably all the aerobic exercise you need during the week. On weekends you can engage in the activities you mention in your letter. Walking, plus more intense aerobic activity on weekends, will quickly pull you out of Dr. Cooper's "poor" category.

A weight training program will round out your prescription for fitness. Weight training will build lean tissue where you once had fat. And you can save yourself time by training at home. You can do a total body workout on a 10-in-1 bench or a multi-station selectorized machine. It'll take you about 30 minutes three times a week.

Finally, schedule yourself for retesting at the Cooper Clinic in six months. This will give you a goal to shoot for and keep you dieting and exercising regularly.

Give fitness a high priority in your life. You'll be glad you did and so will your patients and family.

Priorities

Q. As a lawyer myself, I'm curious how you find time to stay in such excellent shape while engaging in the active practice of law.

A. It's not easy. In addition to my law practice, my Ripped Enterprises mail order business continues to grow and demand more time. Writing books and writing this column take time. My duties as Vice-President of the National Physique Committee take time. I also spend time with my wife, Carol, and my son, Matt. I'm always behind on something, but I nevertheless always find time to train.

It's a matter of priorities. Weight training has always been a top priority item for me. I did some of my best Olympic lifting while I was going through the grind of law school. During my second year in law school I made record lifts right in the middle of final examination week and still ranked number one in my law school class. I think my lifting made the studying easier. Today, my bodybuilding helps me maintain the mental and physical stability I need to keep up with my other responsibilities.

President Carter, who was known for working long hours, took up running while he was in the White House. If you really want to stay in shape you'll find time no matter how busy you are. The rest of your day will be more enjoyable and more productive if you do.

Finding Time To Train

Q. You're a bodybuilder and an attorney, so you'll be familiar with my problem. I want to be the best bodybuilder I can, and I think I have good potential. My bone structure is good, and I have packed on 60 pounds of muscle since high school.

My problem is that I am a second year law student as well as a graduate student in economics. I have to put in so many hours studying that I barely have time to eat and sleep, let alone train. I am interested in economics and law, but they don't hold the same position in my heart as lifting. I suppose part of the reason I am doing it is because I am trying to be the equal of my father, who is a surgeon, and also partly because I don't want to spend my life doing a menial job like some bodybuilders.

School today is so competitive that it leaves little time for anything else. The students I have to compete with think nothing of getting five hours sleep per night or eating once or twice a day (potato chips) or zipping through exam week on bennies. Of course, I can't afford to go to such extremes, which may be to my long-term advantage, but it erodes my short-term competitive edge.

People keep expecting more and more of me as I progress and this means I will have even less time for training. Am I going to have to work even harder once I graduate?

The few professors I have talked to seem to think that I should dedicate my life to law or economics. Once I complained to the Assistant Dean that the workload was interfering with my training. He looked at me like I was a psycho or something.

I am going to have to make some decisions regarding priorities and time management and I don't know quite what to do. I just don't know what to give up—I don't want to give up anything.

This situation has left me deeply frustrated. I would appreciate

The combination of law and bodybuilding has worked well for me. *Photo by Wayne Gallasch.*

any advice you could give me on balancing a professional career with a sport, while maintaining a semblance of a normal family life.

A. I've heard from several law students recently who are having problems similar to yours. As you say, you're going to have to make some decisions regarding priorities and time management. I'll share a few of my own experiences that may help.

I believe training made me a better student. I'm also convinced it makes me more efficient today as a lawyer and in Ripped Enterprises. To give you a simple illustration: I can do more work in the afternoon if I take time out for a 15-minute walk after lunch. Without the walk I feel groggy in the early afternoon.

This also applies on a larger scale. If I take time to train in the morning, I can do more work during the day. If I didn't train, didn't get enough rest and tried to get through the day on coffee and doughnuts, like some of your law school friends and some of my legal colleagues, I wouldn't have as much energy to keep up with my current work load. If you train, eat properly and get enough rest, you'll be able to get more done in the time you have left than you can by trying to study all the time.

There are important parallels between training and studying. In the gym, with high intensity, proper form and good concentration, you can accomplish more in an hour than you can in twice that much time with low intensity, sloppy form and poor concentration. In law school, I found that I could cover a tremendous amount of material if I got up at 4:00 a.m. and studied until time to go to class. There were no distractions, and I started fresh and rested. I did my best studying at that time. I got more out of those early morning hours than from staying up late and putting in twice the time.

I've never been sorry that I took the time to train and eat properly. How you feel about yourself is an important consideration in how effective you are in whatever you do. I wouldn't like facing the world with atrophied muscles and a pot belly, and I don't think you would either. Working out is an integrating factor in my life. If I keep up with my training, I'm able to cope better with other aspects of my life. When things in the gym are looking good, prospects on the outside seem rosier as well.

Sugar Ray Leonard expressed a similar thought in *Sports Illustrated:* "A lot of time, out of training I don't even know where I am. Training gives me sanity. That's the one time in my life when I know what I'm doing." I suspect that was a big part of Sugar Ray's decision to come out of retirement.

I can't conceive of any circumstance that would make me give up training. Oh, sure, my law practice has occasionally forced me to miss a workout, but on the whole I've managed to keep training through thick and thin. I'm sure that you can do the same. When I was in law school I remember asking my father if I would be able to keep up my training when I got into law practice. He said I probably would have more time to train after law school. You'll be happy to hear that he was right.

You may have to rearrange your priorities somewhat and manage your time better, but I don't think you'll find it necessary to give up bodybuilding—in law school or law practice. Remember that Henry Marsh, America's top contender in the 3000-meter steeplechase, made the 1980 Olympic team while going to law school, and in 1983, when he was in law practice, he ran the fastest time in the world since the Moscow Olympics.

Don't worry that your professors and fellow students may not understand. Let them live the way they want to and do the same yourself. I assure you that you needn't spend your life doing menial tasks in order to be a good bodybuilder. You can realize your potential without giving up a career in law or economics.

If you're good enough, you may be able to carve out a lucrative place for yourself in bodybuilding. But don't put all your eggs in one basket until you know you've got what it takes. In my case, I believe being a lawyer has made me a better bodybuilder. In the long run, you may find that's true for you as well.

Training Adds Quality To Living

Q. What are your plans for the future, including competition?

A. I don't feel the competitive urge at the present time, but I don't rule it out for the future. A few years ago my desire to compete provided me with a strong stimulus to train. After I won my height class in the Past-40 versions of Mr. America and Mr. USA, my training goals changed somewhat. This doesn't mean, however, that I no longer have the desire to train hard and improve. To the contrary, at age 45 I have the best physique I've ever had and I'm still strongly motivated to improve. In fact, I get more satisfaction out of my training now than I did when I was younger. Training is an

I get more satisfaction out of my training now than ever before. *Photo by Mike Neveux.*

integral part of my lifestyle. When my bodybuilding goes well everything else seems to fall into place.

Many other people, in and out of bodybuilding, feel much the same way about training. Jane Fonda has studied ballet consistently since her early twenties. No matter where she is or how busy she is, she searches out the best ballet teacher and takes classes. In *Jane Fonda's Workout Book* she says that "at times when everything else in my life seemed to be falling apart, ballet was the constant that ran through my life like a spinal cord, holding it all together, giving it consistency, pulling me through."

Movie producer Richard Zanuck derives a similar satisfaction from running. Zanuck has run almost daily for 20 years. In a recent interview in *Running* magazine, Zanuck said that running helps him cope. It helped him bounce back from two divorces and from being driven out of the presidency of 20th Century-Fox Film Corporation. He formed his own company to produce *Jaws* and *The Sting*. He says, "When those problems were there... the running was so important. Sometimes the run was the only solid thing I could cling to.... There was, and is, great satisfaction in [the] consistency of it."

Like Jane Fonda's ballet and Richard Zanuck's running, bodybuilding improves the quality of my life. This alone would be enough to keep me training hard, but the fact that I'm in a position to inspire other bodybuilders, especially those my age, makes me train harder still. My position as a role model was brought home to me with special force during a recent trip to California.

When I visited World Gym, Joe Gold, the owner, greeted me warmly and then took me over to a group of bodybuilders which included Irvin (Zabo) Koszewski. Pointing to Koszewski, Joe surprised me when he said, "Say hello to the guy you replaced." In addition to being surprised, I was flattered, because Zabo Koszewski was one of my first bodybuilding heroes. When I started training in the fifties, Zabo was a top contender for the Mr. America title and always won the Best Abdominals award.

I recall watching Zabo train his abs at the original Gold's Gym. I can remember my amazement. Koszewski was doing a set of Sit-Ups when I began my leg routine and when I finished, he was still doing Sit-Ups with no break. I don't know how many reps he did, but it was a fantastic number. I later learned that it was customary for him to work his abs daily for half an hour without pause.

It's gratifying to know that I inspire others to add quality to their lives through training. *Photo by Wayne Gallasch.*

239

When I returned home from my recent meeting with Zabo, I got out my copy of Joe Weider's *IFBB Album of Bodybuilding All-Stars* and turned to the section on Irvin Koszewski. It had never occurred to me before, but our physiques do have strikingly similar lines. We are both on the slim side by bodybuilding standards. Abs and legs are our strong points.

I don't think anybody can replace Irvin Koszewski, but I'm delighted that Joe Gold pointed out the similarities in our physiques. The thought that I can inspire other bodybuilders the way Koszewski inspired me gives added purpose to my training.

My meeting with Koszewski gave special meaning to a recent conversation I had with *Muscle & Fitness* editor-in-chief Bill Reynolds, who pointed out that your body mirrors your lifestyle. Diet and training habits can make a remarkable difference in how you look and feel. Bill said to me: "The average 45-year-old man thinks you're incredible, because he looks and feels middle-aged and you look and feel young." I do feel young, and Bill is correct that my diet and exercise habits are largely responsible for my youthful outlook and zest.

Because of the groundwork laid by Joe Weider and other fitness experts, men and women all over the world are learning that sensible diet and exercise make a person look and feel better and, in addition, improves one's self-esteem. As I mentioned earlier, it improves the quality of your life. It gives you confidence and makes you a more productive person. This is why many corporations now encourage their employees to exercise. *The Runner* magazine recently reported that nearly 500 U.S. firms now provide weight rooms and other exercise facilities for their employees. Nearly three times that number make it possible for their workers to use local gyms and other sports centers.

In our own small way, my wife Carol and I are in step with the corporate trend toward exercise facilities at the work place. We've recently become the proud owners of an almost-new building which now houses my law office, Ripped Enterprises and our gym. We have Nautilus machines, pulleys and free weights—the works. A great place to train, it keeps our enthusiasm for bodybuilding sky-high. The gym is primarily for our personal use, but it's also a place where we give bodybuilding instructions on a one-to-one basis.

Muscle & Fitness readers interested in individualized help with their diet and training are welcome to contact us for details.

So no matter whether I compete again soon, I've got every reason to keep training and improving.

Successful Lifestyle

Q. What do you think are the necessary ingredients of a successful lifestyle?

A. In his 1897 treatise, *Is Life Worth Living?*, psychologist and philosopher William James wrote, "Need and struggle are what excite and inspire us; our hour of triumph is what brings the void."

I've found that I'm happiest when I'm working hard to achieve some goal. In my book *Ripped 2,* I said, "It's tremendously satisfying to set a goal, work hard, and then succeed." That's true in bodybuilding and in other activities. It's great to succeed, but working to achieve success is a more lasting process and equally as satisfying.

I believe that the key to a successful happy lifestyle is to constantly set goals for yourself—in bodybuilding, business or whatever—realistic goals, and then work hard to achieve them. Never be content to rest on your laurels. When you achieve one goal, set your sights on a new one.

I enjoy achieving peak condition for a contest or a photo session, but I enjoy the process of moving closer and closer to the goal of peak condition as much or more. The process of losing fat and gaining muscle, getting ripped, is gratifying in and of itself.

If your lifestyle involves constantly working and struggling to achieve something that excites and inspires you, it's successful.

CHAPTER SIXTEEN

THE LAST WORD

CHAPTER SIXTEEN: THE LAST WORD

Advice On Advice

Q. I'm confused. The top bodybuilders offer different and sometimes conflicting advice. Some recommend a low-carbohydrate diet, others a low-fat diet, and still others a balanced, low-calorie diet. Some claim to do up to 75 sets per bodypart while others do as few as 3-4 sets per bodypart. What am I to believe?

A. I'll give you some advice on advice: don't blindly follow anybody's advice. It's almost always a mistake to follow a specific champion's diet and training routine to the letter.

You should analyze advice first to see if it makes sense, and then to see if it applies to your situation. Bodybuilding is a confusing field because there are few hard-and-fast rules. Your common sense will usually allow you to separate good advice from bad. Discard the bad. Take the good and adapt it to your needs.

I've been wrestling with diet and training puzzles most of my adult life; I'm still learning. Rest assured that as you progress in your bodybuilding and gain more experience, you'll find it easier to separate the wheat from the chaff. Keep an open mind. Keep training. And keep thinking.

Most Important Bodypart

Q. If you had to pick one thing as the key to success in bodybuilding, what would it be?

A. My idea of success in bodybuilding isn't winning Mr. Olympia, Mr. America, or Mr. anything. If the title winners are the only successful bodybuilders, then few bodybuilders succeed. Actually, any person who improves his or her body through proper diet and weight training is a successful bodybuilder, as far as I'm concerned.

A bodybuilder should strive to be better each year than the year before. If a title comes along the way, fine. If it doesn't, you still win by moving closer and closer to being the best you can possibly be. Using this criteria, there are thousands and probably millions of successful bodybuilders.

Successful bodybuilding takes determination and hard work, but the real key is the mind. You have to sift through all kinds of conflicting information on diet and training to decide what is best for you. Whatever your bodybuilding goal, you won't achieve it unless you put your mind to it. If your goal is to get ripped, then you must have the mental determination to stick to your diet and your mind must command your body to do a little more each workout, to lift heavier and heavier weights.

Every man and woman reading this magazine can be a successful bodybuilder. The key is to use your most important bodypart—your head.

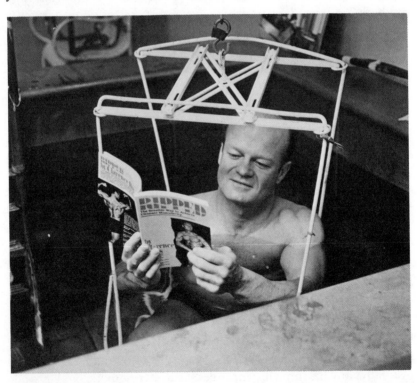

According to Denie, the East Coast editor of *Flex* magazine who took this photo, I'm never without a copy of *Ripped*.

246

This photo and the next two are by John Balik, a master of studio physique photography.

POSTSCRIPT

DO'S AND DON'TS

DON'T:

1. Don't starve yourself or go on a fast, because extreme calorie restriction encourages your body to become fatter.
2. Don't try to lose more than one pound a week, because losing faster will cause a loss of muscle.
3. Don't use a low-carbohydrate diet, because it impairs your ability to think and train properly.
4. Don't eat foods with sugar or fat added or the fiber removed, because they encourage overeating and make you fat.
5. Don't rely on weight training to burn extra calories, because it's too intense and can't be continued long enough to burn a substantial number of calories.
6. Don't try to reduce your waistline with high-volume abdominal exercise, because spot reducing doesn't work.
7. Don't bulk up in the off season, because the muscle you gain is usually lost when you reduce for the next contest.

250

8. Don't eat foods which have sodium (salt) added—this includes almost all processed foods—because they cause water retention and blur your definition.
9. Don't follow your diet too rigidly, because the pressure builds up and eventually causes an eating binge.
10. Don't put more food on the table than you plan to eat, because it's an unnecessary temptation that most people can't resist.

DO:

1. Eat regular well-balanced meals including foods from each of the four major food groups (milk, meat and egg, fruit and vegetable, and bread and cereal).
2. Reduce your caloric intake and increase your activity level just enough to cause a weekly loss of one pound.
3. Eat plenty of whole grains, fruits, and vegetables, because they're filling and satisfying, but low in calories.
4. Use low-intensity, prolonged (30 minutes to one hour) aerobic exercise—walking, jogging, biking, rowing, Heavyhands and rebounding are excellent—to increase your energy expenditure and burn body fat.
5. Exercise all muscle groups with short, high-intensity weight training to build and maintain muscle tissue while you lose fat.
6. Train your waistline just like any other body part, with short, intense workouts.
7. Stay lean in the off season, because the best long-term bodybuilding progress comes when muscle is gained without fat.
8. Eat foods low in sodium and high in potassium—this includes most unprocessed, natural foods—to rid your body of excess water and make your muscles look full and sharply defined.
9. Occasionally eat whatever you crave—ice cream is my main weakness—because it relieves pressure and makes it easier to stay on your diet.
10. Plan your meals in advance and, if possible, purchase only the foods called for by your diet.

PRODUCTS
OFFERED BY
RIPPED™
ENTERPRISES

Have you read
Clarence Bass'
Ripped series,

RIPPED,

RIPPED2 and

RIPPED3 ?

Here's a preview of what's in RIPPED™

RIPPED: The Sensible Way to Achieve Ultimate Muscularity.

RIPPED 2: The all-new companion volume to Ripped.

and... RIPPED 3

The price of **RIPPED** is $10.95, **RIPPED 2** is $13.95 and **RIPPED 3** is $13.95. Please add $1.50 shipping for the first book ($3.00 First Class) and $1.00 for each additional book.

VISA, Mastercard and American Express are welcome. Include card number and expiration date. Credit card holders may also order by phone: 1-505-266-5858 (10 AM to 5 PM Mountain Standard Time, Monday thru Friday.)

NO CANADIAN CHECKS PLEASE. Canadian orders add $4.00 for Air Mail and send U.S. dollars or postal money order in U.S. dollars. Foreign orders, except Canada, add $7.00 shipping for first book and $2.00 (Australia, Africa and Middle East $4.00) for each additional book. Foreign checks must be in U.S. dollars and drawn on a U.S. bank. New Mexico orders add 5% tax.

Order from:

Clarence Bass' RIPPED™ Enterprises
528 Chama, N.E.
Albuquerque, New Mexico 87108

Color Photo. An 8 x 10 shot of Clarence in top shape. Personally auto-graphed to you. Hang it on your wall. It'll inspire you. $5.00 + $1.50 shipping.

Audio Seminar Tapes 1, 2 & 3. Three hour-long tapes in question and answer form (Bill Reynolds, Editor-in-Chief of *Muscle & Fitness* asks the questions) which trace the development of Clarence Bass' Ripped diet and training philosophy. $12.95 each + $1.50 shipping or all three for $30.00 + $1.50 shipping.

Personal Consultations. Telephone, audio cassette, or in person. Call or write for details.

Ripped Recommended Books. The books that helped shape Clarence Bass' *Ripped* diet and training philosophy. Write for current list and prices.

Prompt Shipment Guaranteed. Please add $1.50 shipping for first item ($3.00 first class) and $1.00 for each additional item ordered. NO CANADIAN CHECKS PLEASE. Canadian orders send U.S. dollars or postal money order in U.S. dollars. Foreign orders, except Canada, add $7.00 shipping for first item and $2.00 for each additional item. Foreign checks must be in U.S. dollars and drawn on U.S. bank. New Mexico orders add 5% sales tax. VISA, MASTER-CARD and AMERICAN EXPRESS WELCOME. Include card number and expiration date. Credit card holders may order by phone: 1-505-266-5858 (10 AM to 5 PM Mountain Standard Time, Monday through Friday). Prices subject to change without notice.

Order from:

Clarence Bass'RIPPED™ Enterprises
528 Chama, N.E.
Albuquerque, New Mexico 87108

RIPPED™ Enterprises also offers:

FOOD SUPPLEMENTS—The balanced and complete formula that Clarence takes. Call or write for list and prices.

GYM EQUIPMENT—A complete line of weight training equipment for home and institutional use. Send $2.00 for color catalog and price list.

Call or write for ordering information:

Clarence Bass' RIPPED™ Enterprises
528 Chama N.E.
Albuquerque, NM 87108

(505) 266-5858

10 A.M. to 5 P.M.
Monday - Friday